Managing H

Managing Hotels

Peter Venison

President, Hotel Properties of America

Heinemann : London

William Heinemann Ltd
10 Upper Grosvenor Street, London W1X 9PA

LONDON MELBOURNE TORONTO
JOHANNESBURG AUCKLAND

First published 1983
© Peter Venison 1983

434 92196 3

Printed and bound in Great Britain by
Biddles Ltd, Guildford and King's Lynn

To Diana,
For putting up with an hotelier for so long.

Foreword

The author of this book graduated twenty years ago with a diploma in hotel and catering management from Battersea College of Technology, now the University of Surrey. His class included a number of students who have since been outstandingly successful in their chosen profession. Peter Venison has been one of them. It is, therefore, with particular pleasure that I commend his book, as his former teacher, to a wide audience.

Any teacher should be modest enough to admit that the success of his students in the market place may owe more to themselves than to the course they have taken. It will be readily apparent to the readers of this book how much its author learnt in his twenty years in business. Much of his success has been due to the fact that he has not stopped learning and to the way he has used the work and findings of others to formulate his own approach and management style.

Peter Venison draws on contributions from the behavioural sciences and on his wide experience, to communicate his approach to hotel management in a readable and effective way.

His book is a reaction to much conventional wisdom and accepted practice in his industry and makes a particular challenge to hotel companies and their managers but also to education and training for hotel management. It is concerned above all with the needs of hotel guests and with standards of hospitality, with those who provide and manage that hospitality and the way they go about it; it suggests in a constructive and practical way a re-alignment of attitudes and approaches in the guest–host relationship.

Some are likely to find this book disturbing and some will, no doubt, disagree with much of what is put forward. But none can afford not to read it. Hotel managers and those who manage hotel managers, trainees and students of hotel management, but also those responsible for the education and training of future hotel managers, will find here at least much food for thought, and many are likely to find the message convincing enough to put into practice.

Professor S. Medlik
Formerly Professor and Head of Department of Hotel, Catering and Tourism Management University of Surrey
Currently Visiting Professor and Director Horwath & Horwath (UK) Ltd

Guildford 1983

Preface

If you ever get the chance to meet a group of first year hotel school students and ask them why they have selected hotel keeping for a career, predominant amongst their answers will be the words – 'I like dealing with people'. I am sure that by 'people' what they really have in mind are 'hotel guests' and that they are not really focusing on their forthcoming relationships with colleagues – staff or purveyors. Yet the chances are that by the time they leave the hotel school or college they will have practically forgotten the word 'guest' because it is rarely used in most hotel school syllabi and will have drifted into an environment where 'people' means almost everybody but the guest.

They will certainly be knowledgeable about the creation of a Charlotte Russe, they will be capable of producing a trial balance, they will know what to do with carbon tetrachloride, they will understand the relevant sections of the liquor licensing laws, but they will not have found out much about the needs and desires of the customers – the so-called hotel guests.

Nor will they have a really clear understanding of exactly what a hotel manager does all day. They will know all about what he is supposed to know about and they will know plenty about all the pieces that go together to make the running of an hotel but still no one will have told them exactly what a hotel manager does all day.

I have written this book because it has slowly become apparent to me over twenty years in the industry that this is the sad truth. A truth that is not a theory but a fact. This is not a book about theories; it is a book about my observations and experiences. It is my hope that this slim volume will be read not only by existing practitioners of the hotel industry, but also by the young people who have just embarked on their careers. It is my hope that it will add something to the literature, which is already prescribed or available, and throw a somewhat different emphasis on to the role of hotel management.

What qualifies me, the reader might ask, to express such strong views about the nature of hotel management? What is this 'experience' of which I speak? Happily, I have actually managed an hotel and also managed many managers of hotels. Happily, also, (although often unhappily) I have been the 'guest' of many other hotels throughout the world and have become therefore a professional 'hotel watcher', I have tried not to be specific about an hotel when I wish to use it as an example of something to avoid but here and there the name of a person, company or hotel will unavoidably crop up. I apologise in advance for any offence that may have been given and would ask the offended to forgive me in the light of the purpose of the book.

The other predominant reason for writing this book is my concern for the generally low standards which we, in this industry, ask our customers to accept. How often does one enter an hotel to find stained carpets, nonchalant staff, an untidy atmosphere and generally little pride of appearance? Too often. But these are not the standards that are taught at the hotel schools – in fact the best meal in many towns around the world is the meal you can get at the hotel school restaurant. Where then is the gap; the gap between the standards taught by the schools and colleges and the standards imposed by hotel managers?

This book attempts to explore some of the reasons for the mediocrity in the industry and sets out to suggest a way of managing which, if universally adopted, could restore and maintain higher standards.

The thoughts in this book are not complicated, nor are they original. They have been gathered together from various volumes of behavioural scientists and moulded together with the thoughts of many of my past and present colleagues, bosses and subordinates. There are, of course, many people to thank for the fortunate development of my own career and experiences but three persons in particular bear special mention for their contribution to my career and hence to the material of this book.

First, Alan Marsh, ex-Director of Personnel for H.C.A. (Sonesta) for giving me my head at an early age; secondly George DeKornfeld now General Manager of the Regency Hotel in New York (after a long and interesting career of hotel management) for supporting, teaching and encouraging me once Marsh had got me going and; thirdly, Sol

Kerzner for toughening me up, but also for imparting to me much of his idealism.

Peter Venison

Contents

Foreword 7
Preface 9

1 **An Hotel is a Pyramid**
This chapter examines the behavioural needs of hotel guests and relates them to Abraham Maslow's 'hierarchy of human needs'. It makes the point that, for complete guest satisfaction, needs must be satisfied in a certain order 17

2 **Can't Get 'No' Satisfaction**
Here the distinction between which aspects of hotel service cause satisfaction and which aspects cause dissatisfaction to guests is drawn and a parallel between this and the motivational theories of Frederick Herzberg is cited 25

3 **Administration versus Mobility**
The different poles of hotel management activity are examined and the difficulties of finding human beings who are capable of fulfilling the great range of behaviour demanded by the job of hotel manager is discussed 30

4 **Come out from behind the Chair**
The risks of confrontation and open communication and the processes that are involved are examined in the light of management/guest relationships 35

5 **Model Manager, Model Employees**
An analysis is made of 'how people learn' and the point is made that managers must exhibit 'model' behaviour and set an appropriate example to their employees if they wish their employees to behave correctly 41

6 **Please Tell me Why?**
A discussion on the need to communicate and a focus on the must-know, should-know, would-know analysis of what is to be communicated from manager to employee 48

7 **The Crucial Relationship – Manager to Employee**
A description of the theories of the late Douglas MacGregor, Blake and Mouton, Rensis Likert and others who have researched the relationships which exist between managers and their employees 54

8 **Interfaces and Openings**
The organizational structure of an hotel often ensures that it cannot work properly. This chapter explains the problem of difficult interdepartmental interfaces and describes how these temporarily disappear during hotel 'openings'. 68

9 **Setting 'Goals'**
Hotel management tasks are broken down into marketing, financial, human resource, and standards aspects and some advice is given on how to use this breakdown as a basis for setting achievement goals 73

10 **An Hotel Needs a Team**
A description of one hotel's specific and detailed attempts to build teamwork across interdepartmental lines 78

11 **Being There**
The only effective way an hotel manager can keep on top of his business is to utilize his time in such a way that he gets out of the office and into the 'front line' as much as possible. This gives him the triple benefits of meeting his guests, controlling his standards and getting to know his staff. 86

Contents 15

12 **Don't Just Look – Look and See**
It is simply not enough to manage by being in the thick of the action unless the manager develops observation skills. This chapter examines methods of doing so. 95

13 **Outside Looking In**
To avoid going 'stale' hotel managers should try to look at their operation as an outsider. Managers should also keep abreast of new trends and styles by visiting competitors and by travel. 102

14 **Mobile Control**
The concept of BEING THERE also helps the control function of the hotel since, in the end, physical surveillance plays a major role in hotel control 106

15 **Can the Personnel Function Survive?**
This chapter examines the role of the Personnel Manager in the light of the mobile manager's activity which includes much close contact with his employees 111

16 **The Role of Marketing**
Hotel marketing is really outside the scope of this book because it is not a prime activity of the mobile manager, but it is pointed out that hotel marketing people can also learn something from the behavioural scientists 116

17 **Designing for People**
Hotel design must also take into consideration the requirements of its eventual users – the hotel guest. This chapter initially describes the need for focal points in design where people can meet people. It then goes on to explore the possibilities for future hotel design. 122

18 **Changing Direction**
Some suggestions as to how educationalists and the industry may change the direction of their focus in order to develop more mobile managers 132

Bibliography 137
Index 139

1   *A Hotel is a Pyramid*

During the last twenty-five years the modern hotel business has emerged as a major world industry. Over this period hotel management has become a profession which young people are proud to join and hotel management education has proliferated into a series of courses offering anything from reception lessons to masters degrees in hotel and catering management.

Each year thousands of students enter courses designed to train them for supervision, management or corporate management in the hospitality industry in the USA. Simultaneously hundreds enrol in the UK, countless more in France, Holland, Germany and almost every other country in the world where a hotel industry exists.

Why is it then that in the majority of cases, at least in the western world, standards of hotelkeeping have dropped over the same period? Why have standards of hospitality, professionalism, service, cleanliness, friendliness, and in some cases cuisine, dropped so dramatically over a period when organized training and education for the industry has been on the increase?

This book sets out to examine this phenomena and to suggest changes in patterns of behaviour and maybe education which could have a positive impact on the industry at large. It focuses on the fact that the hotel industry is primarily behavioural, not technical, and as such the behaviour of its employees to its clients and to each other is of fundamental importance. It has been written for the benefit of hotel school students who may not yet have focused on the simplicity of the hotel business and, hopefully, it will fill a gap in the available hotel school textbooks where almost nothing exists in the behavioural area.

Hopefully too, it will be of some interest to seasoned hoteliers, many of whom will also have come to realize that the hotel business consists of a series of simple elements and that management's job is to behave and cause others to behave in such a way that all these simple elements fall together into a complete jigsaw. Most pieces of a jigsaw are simple enough; putting them together requires enormous patience, diligence and attention to detail whilst never losing sight of the complete picture.

Hotels (using the name in its broadest possible sense) can be divided into many different categories – city hotels, resort hotels, motels, cheap hotels, expensive hotels, convention hotels, exclusive hotels, etc., etc. Nevertheless they all have at least one thing in common; they offer bedrooms to rent and in most cases they offer other services related to a human being's needs whilst staying away from home. Most hotel guests (a strange, but nice, word for someone who pays!) are presumably away from home whilst staying in an hotel and all guests have sets of needs that it is the hotelier's task to attempt to satisfy. The hotelier in many cases must endeavour to replace the guests' home – or at least some of the more pleasurable aspects of it and provide replacements related to it whilst the guest is away from it. In short the hotel must often become a 'second home' for the guest.

During the course of this book, the writings, theories and findings of several popular behavioural scientists will be called upon from time to time to illustrate certain themes and thoughts. The hotel student or practitioner should, as part of his training, consider in more depth the findings and research of these behavioural scientists since they will help him to understand more fully the nature of the guest and the nature of the servers of the guest.

The first of these behaviouralists is Abraham Maslow, whose pyramid of the human hierarchy of needs should be studied and understood since it has direct relevance to the needs of hotel guests as well as to the needs of hotel employees. Maslow's hierarchy of needs is often used as a tool in teaching managers to understand the needs of employees and thus create an environment in which they can be managed with more empathy and understanding with a view to better performance.

Maslow, in 1954, postulated a hierarchy of human needs incorporating several levels. Basic to Maslow's theory is the notion that needs at a particular level of the hierarchy must be 'largely' satiated before the needs of the next higher level become operative. This is not to say that two levels cannot be operative at the same time, but the needs at the lower level take precedence.

The basic outline of Maslow's hierarchy from the lowest level to the highest level is as follows.

1 *Physiological needs:* as one might expect these include such things as hunger and thirst.
2 *Safety needs:* these refer primarily to freedom from bodily threat and in our culture are probably most active for young children.
3 *Belongingness or social needs:* these include the need for friendship, affection and love.
4 *Esteem needs:* these represent an individual's need for self respect, for the respect of others, and for a stable, positive evaluation of himself.
5 *Self-actualization needs:* at the top of the hierarchy is the need level most existential in nature and most difficult to define. A succinct definition is simply that an individual's need to self-actualize is the need to be what one wants to be, to achieve fulfillment of one's life goals, and to realize the potential of one's personality.

This theory is very often expressed in the form of this figure.

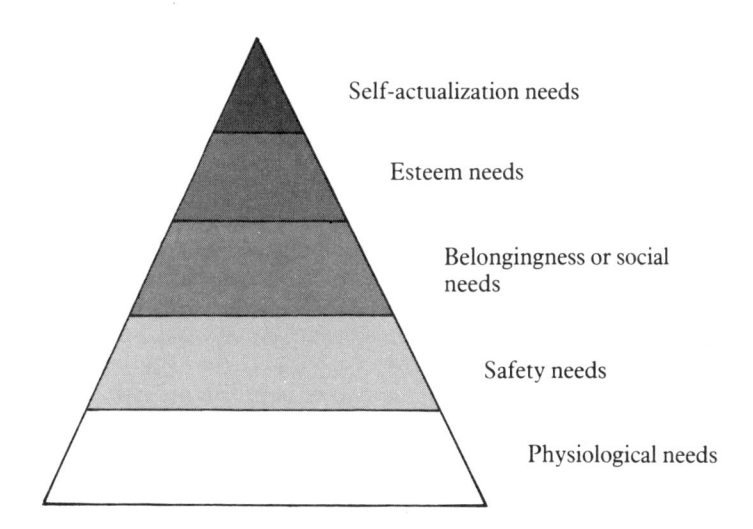

The relevance of the *hierarchy* of needs is probably more graphically illustrated if one imagines primitive man. Without water and food the primitive man would die. If he lacked these items his sole motivation would be to search until he found them, in certain desperate instances throwing all fear aside to capture a source of food. Having found a source of food, albeit temporary, the primitive northern man then satisfied his safety need by seeking shelter from the elements – often a cave – and safety from others or wild animals by fashioning weapons. As we all know, from the safety of his cave he started to learn to cultivate food supplies until his motivation with regard to the base needs began to dim and instead focus on his need to belong. Primitive man obviously set out to find promitive woman but he also started to form social and tribal groupings. One step led to another and the next needs were for bigger and better caves, and more and more effective weapons, and more and more possessions. Primitive man's needs for self-esteem were about to be met and, in a few cases, particularly perhaps with the leaders, maybe even the needs of self-actualization were satisfied.

Why should all this be relevant to the hotel guest? Well, a hotel guest is, of course, a human being with a set of needs which in relation to the hotel should be satisfied in varying degrees by the hotel management. They appear to be obvious needs but are often overlooked by management and not capitalized on by hotel marketing and sales persons.

The basic level of human need on the hierarchy is for sustenance, i.e. to eat and drink; to fill the empty belly. In the caveman example in the description of Maslow's theory, he sharpens his flintstones and rushes off in search of rabbit or buck or whatever else he can catch up with, kill and cook. All hotel guests, sooner or later, look for restaurants, bars or room service. The hotelier who cannot provide these must provide an adequate alternative such as a neighbourhood restaurant or he will fail to satisfy the basic need. Have you ever stayed in an hotel and listened to a resident guest being told that the restaurant is fully booked – particularly with non-residents? He often causes a fuss or goes elsewhere, frustrated. The hotel has failed to satisfy his basic need – even worse, it has ignored *his* basic need in preference for somebody else's.

The next need of the hotel guest is for shelter – a roof over the head under which to rest and recover from the vigours or exertions of the day. Picture the businessman arriving at an hotel after a transatlantic flight or a long car ride. Picture the vacationer from New York arriving in Florida complete with wife and family all eager to enjoy their annual vacation. What are amongst these people's basic requirements? What concern do they share that immediately needs satisfying? To know that they are going to be given a room notwithstanding the fact that they already have a reservation.

Shelley Berman in his excellent book entitled *A Hotel is a Place* points out that the first duty of a front desk clerk is to inform the arriving guest that he has no reservation. How true this can be and what trauma it can cause. The hotelier, therefore, who can honour his promise to provide a room is merely satisfying a basic level of Maslow's hierarchy – fulfilling the need for a roof over the head and relieving concern and anxiety.

Can you imagine the scene whereby an arriving guest gets shown up to a dirty, unmade room or where the plumbing does not work? The basic need is not met – often with disastrous consequences.

However, most hotels do manage to satisfy these fundamental guest requirements, at least to a reasonable degree but it is from here on that 'the men are separated from the boys'.

Refer again to our caveman. Having housed, clothed and fed himself what did he look for ? A mate, friends, love? An atmosphere to call a home – a place to feel wanted, loved, to belong.

Is this different for the hotel guest? Not at all.

His next requirement is just that – to feel at home – or at least in a home away from home. It is so important and meaningful for the hotel guest to receive a warm and friendly greeting, to be addressed by his name, to be remembered, to be dealt with in sincerity and to feel hospitality. By achieving this atmosphere the hotelier is merely satisfying the next human need on the Maslow pyramid.

What next for the caveman? That's right, he becomes materialistic. He wants a bigger and better cave, more comfortable, more convenient – something to make the caveman neighbours say 'wow'!

And the hotel guest? You've got it – a swankier address, a larger room, a grander lobby, an interior designed atmosphere – the 'Ritz'. In the restaurant the customer does not simply want to satisfy hunger, he wants to experience the delights of haute cuisine, the graciousness of the service, and the pride of being at the right address.

So what is hotelkeeping all about? It is about satisfying the needs of its customers, needs which are remarkably close to the general life needs of human beings described so simply by Abraham Maslow.

Many other industries and businesses have studied and learned from Maslow and similar researchers of human needs. The clothing industry and the automobile industry for example have learnt to satisfy basic needs but exploited higher ones. But no industry so closely parallels the complete human hierarchy of needs as does the hotel industry because satisfying a range of human needs is precisely the task of the hotelier.

This book will examine ways of managing hotels to satisfy the needs beyond the truly basic levels and of ensuring that they are satisfied in the correct order if they cannot all be met. Note carefully that the need to be 'loved' and welcomed comes before the need for self-esteem in the pyramid as well as for the need for greater material possessions. That is why the most extravagantly designed hotels in the most fashionable areas can often fail if the staff attitude is not correct. How many times have you heard the comment that an hotel is splendid in design but that it is 'cold'? Magnificent lobbies do not necessarily satisfy guests. It is fundamental in Maslow's research findings that each level of human needs must be substantially satisified before the next one can be reached. An hotel, therefore, with a magnificent design will fail, if it relies on, in any form, repeat business, if it is not satisfying the human need on the rung beneath.

How, in the context of Maslow, has the world's hotel industry changed over the last quarter of a century and what have been the results? This question will be dealt with in more detail later, but consider a few major factors at this stage.

The Size of Hotels

Hotels for a period of time became larger and larger. The hotel industry had its foundation in small inns and lodging houses. For economic reasons apparently hotels became bigger and bigger. Once the developers had paid for the site and the infrastructure it became economic sense to add as many rooms as possible. It did not, however, necessarily make behavioural sense from a guest's point of view and the developers of large hotels lost sight of the human need of being 'loved and wanted'. As we have all heard before 'in x hotel you feel like a number'. This complete ignoring of the needs of guests by developers did, in fact, severely set back the standards of hotelkeeping.

Recent developments in the US spearheaded by the growth of John Colman's emergent Fairfax, Navarro, etc. chain plus the unveiling of Hyatt's 'small hotel' concept seem to indicate that the lesson has been learned and that the trend has been reversed.

The Chain Hotel

The international and national hotel chains were formulated over this period and it was certainly not just good fortune that caused Intercontinental and Hilton, two of the original worldwide chains, to be successful.

Who were the bulk of the customers? Travelling Americans. Why choose Hilton or Intercontinental when the Georges Cinq and the Vier Jarvietzeiten existed? Because the less sophisticated travellers, which included most, knew they would satisfy their basic human needs by this choice. They were safe! They knew that they could expect a bed, a room, and a steak just like those back home. Certainly the need for the 'cave' was satisfied and the belly could be safely filled with familiar food and even the surety that the hotel staff would speak English assured the traveller of similarities with home which at least started to satisfy the next rung of human need.

That is not to say, of course, that had the traveller ventured to new strange pastures of the Georges Cinq or the Vier Jarvietzeiten he would not have been equally satisfied but the traveller could never be sure in advance. They therefore opted for the choice that assured them that they would satisfy at least the basic needs.

Gradually, of course, as they found that the Hilton and the Intercontinental and its American emulators satisfied only their basic needs they moved on to perhaps the 'better' addresses of the George Cinq, etc. to satisfy their self-esteem but it is interesting to note that, true to Maslow, the lower needs had to be satisfied before the higher ones.

The Fantastic Design of Hotels

Another phenomenon of the last decade or two has been the amazing architectural wonders that have been created as hotels. Hyatt in particular have very successfully built up a splendid reqution for architectural impact. Westin, Omni and others have followed suit. Whilst it is difficult to argue with the success of this philosophy it is possible according to the hierarchy of Maslow that all the expense of the structures will not pay dividends since it appeals to the upper levels of human need satisfaction when the lower ones, particularly those of love and companionship may not yet have been fulfilled. All the expense of a 'John Portman' lobby can be lost completely on a customer if the desk clerk is rude to him - and in any event, once one has seen an architectural feature one has seen it - whereas human contact is somehow renewable.

A possible contribution therefore to the demise of good hotelkeeping has been the fact that some hoteliers went out to satisfy the higher needs on the hierarchy and either ignored or failed to satisfy the lower ones first or on a continuing basis. It is, of course, inexpensive to satisfy the human need to be 'wanted' whereas it is very costly to attempt to satisfy all his needs for self-esteem. It is, however, easier on an ongoing basis to take the costlier route since 'wanting' somebody needs to be worked at continuously.

The foregoing, of course, is an oversimplification and the various factors which will satisfy one individual in an hotel will not necessarily satisfy another, but in general terms Abraham Maslow's hierarchy of needs is a good road map for the hotelier and hotel developer to follow. His research into human needs is a good guideline for the hotelier to note. In short - a clean comfortable room with a good bed, a simple meal and a smile from the staff can go a long way further than the most modern facilities with unfriendly staff. Future chapters examine what hotel managers must do to satisfy or organize others to satisfy the needs that have been discussed here.

2 *Can't Get 'No' Satisfaction*

Whilst Abraham Maslow's theories of the needs of human beings seem to relate so closely to the needs of hotel guests, so do the findings of another famous industrial behavioural researcher – Frederick Herzberg.

Herzberg is best known for his hygiene/motivation theory which is widely taught in man-management courses. The classical approach to motivation, according to Herzberg, has concerned itself with the environment in which the employee works; i.e. the circumstances that surround him while he works and the things he is given in exchange for his work. Herzberg considers this concern with the environment to be an ongoing necessity of management, but that it is not sufficient in itself for effective motivation. Motivation requires experiences that are inherent in the job itself.

Herzberg maintains that it is impossible to motivate people by utilizing environmental factors, i.e. better conditions of work (he calls them *hygiene* factors). Only through achieving satisfaction from the job itself can people, he maintains, be fully motivated with lasting effect.

He uses the term hygiene to describe such things as physical working conditions, supervising policies, the climate of union-management relations, wages and fringe benefits. Herzberg chose the term *hygiene* to describe these factors because they are essentially preventative from the environment, just as trash removal removes threats to health from the physical environment. His research has shown that when any of these factors are deficient, employees are quite likely to be displeased and to express their displeasure in ways that hamper the organization, e.g. through grievances, decreased effort or even strikes. When the deficiencies are corrected productivity may return to normal but is unlikely to rise above that level. In other words, an investment in hygiene may eliminate a deficit, but it does not create a gain. As Herzberg says 'Just as eating a meal does not prevent a man from becoming hungry in the future, a wage increase will not prevent him from becoming dissatisfied eventually with his new wage level'.

To sustain higher levels of performance an employee must be motivated and motivation according to Herzberg describes the feelings of accomplishment, of professional growth and professional recognition, that are experienced in a job that offers sufficient challenge and scope to a worker.

Thus Herzberg has illustrated to thousands of managers that 'dissatisfiers' are not the opposite of 'satisfiers' – they are just different. The lessons to be learned from Herzberg's research and theories are, of course, applicable to the management of hotel employees and the structuring of hotel jobs – and many hotel education programmes refer in some depth to Herzberg's work in their man-management syllabi.

They do not, however, focus, once again, on the parallels of Herzberg's theory to the satisfaction of the guest and just as many managers spend time trying to motivate their employees by focusing on the wrong processes (i.e. hygiene factors), many more spend their time trying to satisfy guests without understanding the difference between satisfiers and dissatisfiers.

For example, do you think an arriving hotel guest will be dissatisfied if his hotel room is to be dirty? Of course he will! On the other hand do you think an arriving hotel guest will be satisfied if he arrives in a clean room? No – he will not be satisfied; he will just not be dissatisfied!

Similarly, whereas the provision of soap and towels in an hotel room does not satisfy the average hotel guest; the lack of soap and towels is certain to cause dissatisfaction.

Below are two questions and extracts from two lists which I have tested informally on many people. Try answering the questions for yourself to see if your own results confirm my experiences which are marked accordingly.

1 The items listed below are all unfavourable aspects of an hotel operation. Give each item a rating as to the amount of dissatisfaction it will cause a guest.

	Dissatisfaction		
	High	Medium	Low
A reservation mix up upon arrival		■	
Dirty bedroom	■		
Rather sullen staff		■	
Insufficient bathroom linen	■		
Inefficient wake-up service		■	
Only 'average' food		■	
Staff do not address guest by name			■
Insufficient supply of hot water	■		
Manager never seen			■
Hotel decoration rather ordinary			■
Public areas are quite 'dead'			■

2 The items listed below are all favourable aspects of an hotel operation. Give each item a rating as to the amount of satisfactory impact it would have on a guest.

	Satisfaction		
	High	Medium	Low
A correctly handled reservation			■
A clean room		■	
Ever-smiling, courteous employees	■		
Sufficient towels			■
Efficient wake-up service		■	
Excellent food	■		
Many staff remember your name	■		
Sufficient supply of hot water			■
Manager makes contact with guests	■		
The hotel is strikingly decorated		■	
The public areas of the hotel are lively and full of people		■	

If your results with this experiment are similar to mine, by 'overlaying' in your mind one list on top of the other, you will have a clear indication about satisfiers and dissatisfiers from the movement of your markings. This appears to reaffirm the findings of Maslow as described in Chapter 1, i.e. unless the factors on the lower level of human needs are met you have no chance of satisfying the upper level needs. In our adaptation of Herzberg's theory it is clear that unless the *hygiene* or environmental factors affecting a hotel guest are met then he will be dissatisfied because the hotel has failed to achieve even the minimum standards required. On the other hand it is apparent that by achieving minimum standards one merely removes cause for dissatisfaction – one does not automatically give satisfaction.

The hotel manager therefore who believes that, because he receives no complaints about his services, all his guests are satisfied could be fooling himself. A guest will be truly satisfied when he 'feels the warmth'.

3 *Administration versus Mobility*

As one progresses through a hotel career one frequently encounters hotel managers who say that 'you cannot get good staff any more' – and that staff are disinterested in the job and that for these reasons it is impossible to give good service any longer. It is, of course, true that people, and therefore employees, have changed – in different degrees in different countries, but cultural changes that have characterized modern-day society seem to be accelerating at an ever-increasing rate. The effects of different forms of education and a different life-style of the young affect all organizational life. Each succeeding generation at least during this century seems to be raised in a somewhat more permissive climate than the last and as a result younger employees seem to have stronger needs for independence and self respect and far less tolerance for another's behaviour. They do not respond so well to the simple economic and security needs on which their fathers' depended, particularly since in many countries social welfare has made it almost as profitable not to work as to work.

In short, today's worker cannot often be motivated to work well simply by being told to do so. The manager apparently cannot just rely on workers to get on with the job. He must himself manage in such a way that motivates others on his payroll. He must understand and utilize the motivation factors touched upon in the last chapter.

One will also hear that 'old-time' employees had more pride in their jobs than youngsters. Much of this can be attributed to changing cultures but can any of the blame be laid at the feet of the management? Has hotel management changed over the last few decades and if so how and with what effect?

The origins of the modern hotel industry are still recognizable in the grand old hotels of Europe. In Switzerland for example the traditions of hotelkeeping were firmly established around the turn of the century and in many instances have changed little. Before the conglomerates and hotel chains, most hotels, even ones that were large for the times (although small, of course, compared with today's standards) were owned by individuals or partnerships. Owners very often worked in the businesses themselves and kept a close eye on things. Hotels that were successful developed very close contact between owner and customers. We all can recognize the self-esteem that is created for the guest who is greeted by an owner rather than a manager. However, in many cases managers were hired but the scope of the work was often limited, for very good reasons, to the supervision of 'operations' and the contact with the customer. Another individual, normally of equal status in the eyes of the owner, was hired to 'control' the business. The public, of course, never met this individual. To them, the all-important figure was the hotel manager who had to act with great diplomacy and dignity in his display of concern about the well-being of his guests. The division of management between 'operations' and 'control', long since abandoned by the US trained hotel manager, was founded, of course, on a fundamental understanding of the needs of the client (i.e. the maintenance of standards and the need to be 'wanted') and a realization that no one man could cope properly with all that and the administrative control of the business.

As an eager young personnel manager in Europe in the 1960s I remember well being confused by this dual management concept of the traditional European hotelier. I had received my training through a formal management course and had thereafter joined an American hotel company. Upon being given the brief to recruit managers for some new American hotels in Europe, I found it exceptionally difficult to find qualified individuals who possessed the broad range of general management experience and abilities laid down by my American masters. The top candidates almost invariably were exceptionally well trained 'front' men or exceptionally well trained 'admin' men but never any that could handle both roles. Furthermore, at that time, the premier European Continental hotel schools were continuing to train students to be hoteliers rather than businessmen, whereas the Americans were hard at work developing businessmen rather than hoteliers. Few seemed to be concerned with producing business-oriented hoteliers!

Now, when I interview hotel managers for management positions I ask them to pinpoint their own management style on the scale described below:

```
┌───┬───┬───┬───┬───┬───┬───┬───┬───┐
1   2   3   4   5   6   7   8   9   10
```

Excessively administrative type of manager. Spends much time on systems planning, accounting and control-orientated work. Rarely leaves his office. Is uncomfortable in sales, public relations activities.

Excessively mobile and promotions-orientated manager. Meets many people. Sociable, spends plenty of time in public areas, as well as behind the 'scenes' of the action. Joins in freely with guests. Is bored by routine and administration.

Most respondents place themselves between 3 and 4 or between 6 and 7 indicating that the two distict ends of the simple scale are clearly recognizable and that most people see themselves with leanings in one direction or the other and that it is obviously bad to be completely at 1 or completely at 10. It does seem that hotel managers can be 'placed' at different points upon the line.

The ideal hotel manager, of course, does not sit at any one point on the scale permanently. The ideal manager is able to flow freely from one end of the scale to the other with complete ease as the requirements on the manager change which they do with every new occurrence. The ideal hotel manager, however, probably does not exist and by correctly assessing what my respondents have confirmed by their answers on the scale, the Swiss hotel owners of years gone by had obviously recognized that the range of human behaviour required from one hotel manager was too broad for any one person to handle – hence the creation of two managers – one hotel manager 'front' and one 'administrative controller'.

Which one became famous and sought after? The front man of course – and the process, therefore, made it more of an 'honour' for the guest to be met by the 'manager'. And just how did this method of satisfying the upper levels of the human need ensure that at the same time the fundamentals were achieved? By the nature of his work the manager in meeting his guests had to be where most of the guests were, i.e. at the busiest points of service. By *being there* the manager could quickly see the trouble spots and correct them before they became disasters. By *being there* the manager could see which employees worked well and which did not, he could get to know them and they could learn from him. *Being there* turned out to be very important and this style is more closely examined in Chapter 11.

What happened to the Swiss system? What happened was that the nature of the hotel industry changed. The conglomerates and the chains took over the world and hotels became larger and larger, requiring more and more specialized systems of control. Hotel management education became more and more sophisticated and less and less concerned with the fundamental needs of the guests as it became more and more concerned with the fundamentals of controlling the business. Hotel 'owners' as individuals began to disappear and were replaced by area vice-presidents, senior vice-presidents and boards of directors. Managers were bombarded with specialists from central office; specialists in computer programming, specialists in marketing, specialists in training and, of critical importance, specialists in producing paper. Hotel management courses sprung up in the western hemisphere designed to teach hotel managers to be economists, accountants, advertising executives, dieticians and to teach them how to deal with other such specialized persons with whom they would have to relate. In short, the focus of hotelkeeping started to become more and more administrative and since these same practitioners of management theory prescribed that there could only be a span of control of seven, the dual structure reporting to the owner disappeared and the hotel general manager (Jack of all trades – master of none) was born.

The hotel general manager has an impossible task to perform because it is generally beyond the behavioural range of most human beings and the sufferer has been the hotel guest – since guest contact and, to a large degree, staff contact have often been lost in the process. And it is right here that the question posed earlier of 'how have changes in hotel management style reduced the feelings of pride in the jobs of employees?' can be answered, since the loss of contact between management and employee is a key element, which will be examined in the next chapter.

Before moving on, however, take a moment to consider once again your own position on the one to ten scale described earlier. Do you naturally fall to the left or to the right? Despite your natural position on the scale are you able to push yourself into behaviour, which is at first unnatural to you? On what range of the scale do you feel comfortable? The trick of being a perfect hotel manager is to be comfortable at all positions on the scale, so obviously the more successful you can be at extending your area of comfort on the scale the more complete a hotel manager you will be. How can you stretch yourself up and down the scale? By taking risks, i.e. risks with your own behaviour. And by practising behaviour that is difficult for you.

I have been fortunate enough to witness several young managers who, prior to their promotion to manager, had been regarded as 'quiet' or 'shy' or 'administratively' oriented. Thrown in at the deep end and confronted with 'guest' situations many of these have been able to experiment with their behaviour and gain so much confidence that their whole personalities have become broader and more interesting.

4 *Come out from behind the Chair*

In early 1981 one of the greatest practitioners of the art of hotelkeeping died in Hamburg, Germany. His name was Albert Elovic and he will be long remembered by all who worked with him (nobody ever worked 'for' him) and by many thousands of hotel guests. Albert's age at death was indeterminable but what was certain was that he had possibly managed a greater variety and number of hotels than any other living man. Canada, the United States, the Caribbean, Bermuda, Israel, Germany, Italy were all countries where he had been an hotel manager and possibly many more. Albert was a creator – an exceptionally active person who believed in taking on a challenge, getting it right – and then moving on to the next one. He was the ultimate behavioural hotel management model. He spoke and read fluently eighteen languages. He was a terrific communicator and an enormous personality.

In November 1980 I made a detour on a business trip to renew my friendship with Albert who at the time had taken on the task of 'renovating' the fabric and the personnel of a magnificent but tired and poorly run hotel near Porto Banus, Spain. Albert had been there six months – during which time he had learned Spanish so that he could 'communicate'.

The staff of the hotel who had apparently previously been very surly (you will recall the disastrous labour problem in the Spanish hotel industry in 1978 and 1979) were eating out of Albert's hand and the bookings for the hotel were pouring in at an uncharacteristically high rate. It was obvious that Albert, after six months, had completely changed the direction of the hotel. Yet, all along the coast, were other hotels in semi-closed, run down conditions, where such a turnaround was not apparent.

I spoke with Albert about his style. I asked him his secret. 'My secret, my boy, is that I've got guts, I talk to my guests and I talk to my staff and it takes guts to do that. Most young managers I know haven't got the guts to meet their clients – they are frightened about what they will hear. Unless I hear what's wrong I can't put it right and I can't use my charm on people to make them forget'.

Albert spent his life talking and listening to his guests and staff. He got great pleasure from his work and he gave great pleasure.

The importance of 'contact' also came home to me (very forcibly) on another occasion. A few years ago my wife and I were fortunate to go on a round-the-world trip which took us from Johannesburg to Mauritius, India, Thailand, Singapore, Hong Kong, North Korea, Taiwan, Japan, Hawaii, USA, France and back to Johannesburg. The trip was fundamentally a vacation but since we were to be in each location for two to three days I was determined to try to learn something *en route* from other hoteliers and we, therefore, opted to stay in good hotels. I made my reservations personally by letter on my hotel company letterhead well in advance. I did not ask for or mention discounts. If I recall correctly we stayed at twelve hotels *en route* and to my complete surprise and dismay we did not meet one hotel manager. Not only did we not meet one but we did not see one. I did not go to the desk to ask for the manager but I did spend plenty of time observing what went on in each location and learned many useful things about design, concept and equipment. In two hotels the managers had left a bowl of fruit in our room – one with a printed card and one with a handwritten note of welcome, which was nice – and in one hotel we were met at the airport with a hospitality car and a public relations lady who had used her initiative and made a hairdressing appointment for my wife.

As we went up in the elevator to our room in that particular hotel my wife turned to me and said 'You know, I think we're going to like it here'. As it happened everything went wrong with the service at this place – but somehow we forgave all because of the human 'contact'.

Shelley Berman has obviously experienced the phenomena of the hiding manager. In 'A hotel is a place' he describes the manager and the assistant manager in the following manner.

Is the case of the disappearing hotel manager due to lack of guts as Albert Elovic claimed or is it due to organizational pressures which keep managers away from the front line? Part of the answer is, of course, that people like to do what they feel comfortable doing which would seem to indicate that many modern hotel managers, as Albert suggested, do feel uncomfortable in meeting guests or alternatively perceive it as a waste of time.

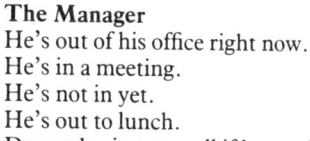

The Manager
He's out of his office right now.
He's in a meeting.
He's not in yet.
He's out to lunch.
Do not hesitate to call if he can be of any assistance, or contact the Assistant Manager.

The Assistant Manager
He's out of his office right now.
He's in a meeting.
He's expected any moment.
He's out to lunch.
Do not hesitate to call him if he can be of any assistance.

Consider the simple figure, known as the Johari window, which demonstrates some of the processes involved in communications.

	I know	I don't know
You know		
You don't know		

When two people meet for the first time they probably know very little about each other and their range of communication is likely to be very superficial and limited. The only area of common knowledge that they have fills the upper left-hand corner of the Johari window. It is safe to talk about things that I know you know about me and vice versa. This is the level at which much superficial conversation remains at between hotel manager and guest. Talk tends to revolve around usual common 'knowns' such as the weather or the sports results.

The only way for communications between two persons to expand out of the top left-hand corner is if one party or the other 'risks' sharing some information or feelings that the other party does not yet know.

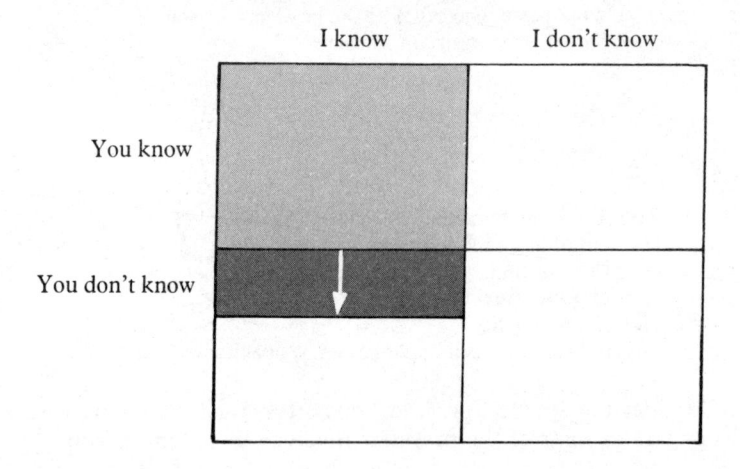

	I know	I don't know
You know		
You don't know	↓	

By taking the plunge and 'sharing' with you I am expanding the area of communication into the lower left-hand corner of the window. I do, of course, take a risk. You may not be interested in what I say, you may think it is ridiculous, you may use it against me, etc., etc. One thing is for certain, however, and that is that unless you are a very low reactor you are likely to respond and your very response will tell me something about you that I had not previously known, thereby moving into the upper right-hand corner of the window (see below).

The interesting fact is that when one party gives information or shares feelings the other usually reacts by doing the same, thereby continually widening the area of common knowledge and the depth and breadth of communication.

	I know	I don't know
You know		
You don't know		

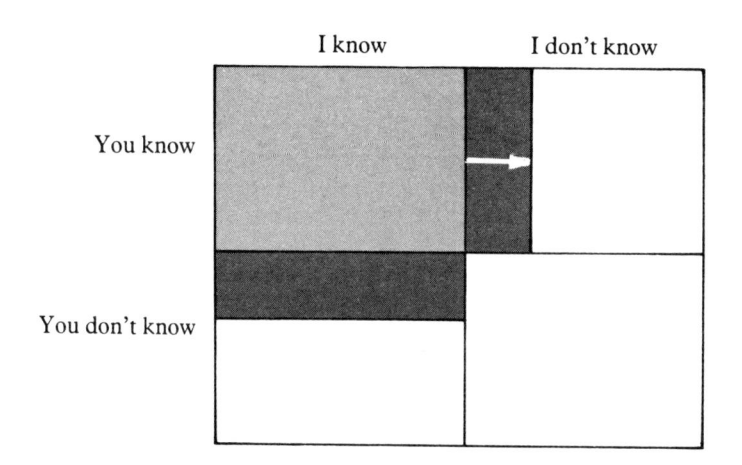

The more one pushes into the areas of sharing feelings the more 'guts' one needs, because people do find it tough to share feelings, but the greater the shaded area becomes in the 'window' the greater understanding there will be between the two parties and the greater potential for them to sort out problems and conflict between themselves.

What is important about all this and what is particularly relevant to the hotel manager is that somebody has to start the process of expanding the shaded portion. Many, many hotel guests with perfectly legitimate reason to complain do not like to do so – or, as is obvious from the foregoing, complain to the front desk clerk because the manager is 'in a meeting', 'out to lunch', etc. (One of the best ways for a manager to find out about how well his hotel is functioning is to eavesdrop at the cashiers' desk.)

The onus of starting the communication, therefore, is clearly on the manager and he must summon up the necessary energy and 'guts' to do so. He cannot do this from his office. By the time a complaint reaches his office the complaint is so ancient or the complainer is so aggravated that no amount of good communication will make the customer come back – especially if he has had to search for the manager in the first place.

Managers must organize their lives so that they can make guest contact frequently and those managers who find it difficult or uncomfortable must understand the fundamental importance of 'contact'. They should also understand that 'practice makes perfect'. Things, which at first are uncomfortable, become more and more comfortable and easy to deal with as one practices them. The first time that a hotel manager is called to greet the Prime Minister he naturally feels nervous. If the instance recurs he will feel less nervous and so on until he feels comfortable.

The other important fact to remember is the sincerity with which one communicates. Sincerity begets sincerity. Insincerity begets insincerity. Deceit begets deceit. If the hotel manager deals with a guest in a sincere manner he demonstrates to the guest that he really cares about the guest and the guest's needs and even the most troubled or irate guest will leave impressed and willing to give the establishment a second chance.

The importance of broadening areas of communication affects all of us in our everyday lives just as the same process between countries affects our peaceful co-existence. It is of paramount importance in the hotel industry and it appears to have been frequently forgotten.

Of course we must recognize that the hotel manager cannot possibly make contact with all around him every day but that, in any event, by doing his 'bit' he will be displaying modelling behaviour which will rub off on to others. Some companies have, however, recognized the crucial importance of 'contact' and built up their organizations accordingly.

Many have utilized 'lobby' managers or public relations officers to make the contacts. This is generally a good idea if it is in addition to the manager playing his role – not instead of. One successful company, Club Mediterranee, has been brave enough to create a whole new breed of hotel employees – as G.O's (general operators) – and a hotel of 200 rooms can have as many as 30 of them on the payroll. They are not normally hotel trained staff but are often university students, writers, actors, etc. Their sole task appears to be to mix with the guests to the extent of drinking with them, playing sport with them, eating with them, generally making sure that they have a good time.

Surely the ultimate in guest contact? But a formula that has worked. Club Mediterranee is one of the success stories of the last decade and it has been so because its conceptual and organization design was put together after its President had taken a thorough look at what people look for (i.e. what are people's needs) at a resort hotel. The level of repeat business achieved by Club Mediterranee is staggeringly high.

5 Model Manager, Model Employees

To get hotel employees to perform in a manner that will result in the satisfaction of guests' needs, particularly those upper level needs, which depend on the behaviour of the hotel employees, these employees must, of course, first know what they are supposed to do and be motivated to do it.

If one, therefore, as a manager wishes to have the employees do what they are supposed to do then it is up to one to teach them. And since that is the case one should have an understanding of how people learn – a subject on which there has been much behavioural research.

There are two areas in which employees can learn; off the job in a classroom or training session or whilst actually performing the job. With regard to learning skills, both physical and interpersonal rather than merely learning 'information', most research indicates that classroom type learning is achieved in four steps:

1. *Modelling*, in which correct behaviour, i.e. 'model behaviour' is demonstrated either by the trainer or by some other method such as a tape or film;
2. *Role playing*, in which the trainees take part in extensive rehearsal of the behaviour demonstrated by the models during which time they receive:
3. *Social reinforcement* (praise, reward, constructive feedback), from other trainees as their role play behaviour becomes more and more similar to the models. These three steps are implemented in such a manner that:
4. *Transfer of training*, from classroom to job setting is encouraged.

Classroom training does, of course, have a limited place in the hotel world but is particularly necessary in the teaching of basic skills which are required to satisfy the fundamental and lower level needs of the guest, e.g. cooking and cleaning. When it comes to satisfying the next level of needs, however, the learning requirement is behavioural and interpersonal and what better laboratory for experimentation than actually on the job? But who will play the trainer's role if the learning is to be achieved on the job? Answer: management, i.e. management at all levels with each level setting the models, watching the real life 'role play' and providing constructive feedback to all levels of employee for whom he or she is responsible.

For those who would like a more in-depth, yet simply-presented, analysis of learning processes I can suggest that you read *Changing Supervisor Behaviour* by Goldstein and Sorcher – Pergamon Press, 1974.

In their book Goldstein and Sorcher point out that although people learn by copying others (models) they seem to do so in a discriminating manner. In other words it is clear people learn from modelling under some circumstances but not in others. Behavioural research has identified certain conditions which seem to enhance the chance of successful learning through observation of 'models' and these conditions are described by Goldstein and Sorcher as follows.

Model characteristics
Greater modelling will occur when the model (the person to be imitated), in relation to the observer: (*a*) is of apparent high competence or expertness, (*b*) is of high status, (*c*) controls resources desired by the observer, (*d*) is of the same sex and race as the observer, (*e*) is apparently friendly and helpful, and, of particular importance, (*f*) when the trainee is rewarded for engaging in the depicted behaviour. That is, we are all more likely to model powerful but pleasant people who receive reinforcement for what they are doing, especially when the nature of such reinforcement is something that we too desire.

Modelling display characteristics
Greater modelling will occur when the modelling display depicts the behaviour to be modelled: (*a*) in a vivid and detailed manner, (*b*) in order from least to most difficult behaviours, (*c*) with sufficient frequency and repetitiveness to make overlearning probable, (*d*) with a minimum of irrelevant detail, and (*e*) when several different models rather than a single model are utilized.

Observer characteristics
Greater modelling will occur when the observer is: (*a*) instructed to model, (*b*) similar to the model in relevant attitudes or background, (*c*) favourably disposed towards or attracted to the model, and, most important, (*d*) rewarded for engaging in the modelled behaviour.

If, therefore, a hotel manager is keen for his employees to behave in a manner that will satisfy his customers' needs he should examine the model characteristics described above carefully because it would appear that he is the 'number one model' and his own behaviour therefore is of paramount importance.

When I was in my early twenties I worked as Personnel Manager at a large luxury hotel in the West End of London. I had a great respect for my General Manager but often found, from my role of Personnel Manager, his behaviour to be frustrating. For example, one of my responsibilities at the time was to design and implement an employee pension plan, the details of which had to be approved by, first, my General Manager and thereafter the central office of the company. I got particularly frustrated in trying to review the details with the General Manager because every time we sat down in his office to do so he would keep jumping up and down on visits to the front desk. He was, of course, going to meet and greet arriving and departing guests. This General Manager had set himself a rigid target of meeting at least ten arrivals per day come what may. Each day he took the arrivals list for the following day and underlined ten names. This underlined list was returned to the front desk and receptionists were instructed to call the General Manager every time one of the underlined guests arrived, at which point he would go to greet them irrespective of whatever else he was doing at the time.

His behaviour irritated me intensely but I could not criticize it because not only was he personally meeting many guests and, therefore, satisfying their needs but, more important, he was modelling and it did not take long for all his assistant managers, including myself, to underline our ten names on the list and perform in a similar manner until at least one-third of all our guests were met by management upon arrival.

Another trait which this particular General Manager had was to pick up litter. He would not walk down a corridor or across a lobby without him at some point or other stooping to pick up the most minute piece of paper or cloakroom ticket or whatever had not found its way to the litter bin. Soon every member of staff was racing the next to pick up litter as soon as it was discarded. This may seem obvious and trite but several years later in my career I visited a famous modern hotel in Paris where they were proud of the most advanced computer system regarding reservations, room service, billing, controls, etc. The Assistant Manager showed me round the place and I couldn't help but notice that the hotel was grubby. Ashtrays were full, the carpets were stained, uniforms were tired, etc. I asked him about the background of the hotel manager and he explained to me that the manager had been a computer programmer. Apparently the systems had become far too complex for the normal hotel manager and since they had been so expensive to install the owners had finally resorted to hiring a computer specialist as the top man. At that point I thought of my old litter picking manager and smiled. I was certain which one I thought was best, but it was interesting to see how the model behaviour of the manager in each case affected the style of the employees and the standards of the hotel.

Let us examine therefore the model characteristics and apply them to our hotel manager. 'Greater modelling will occur when the person to be imitated *is of apparent high competence or expertness'*. An employee is obviously not going to copy a manager who clearly is less able or expert in the task than the employee himself. Since the technical skills of hotelkeeping are limited (mainly to the skills required in the kitchen and to a lesser degree in restaurants) this should not present a major problem to the properly technically trained manager. The basic levels of physical skills, as opposed to behavioural skills, can present a problem to the 'university' trained hotel manager rather than the on-the-job or 'technical school' trained manager, and it is for this reason that hotel managers who were trained at the Lausanne Hotel School with its high emphasis on technical skills find it easier to be 'models' than managers trained at the hotel management universities. On the other hand hopefully the 'university' manager should have a better understanding of the theories of applied learning and the pschychological needs of the customers and should therefore be able to perfect better modelling on the interpersonal levels – although what has actually to be done is very, very simple and certainly does not require a 'degree' to be successfully achieved.

High status
It is for this reason that proper behaviour modelling must start at the top. The Managing Director of a large hotel chain was once heard to express frustration that his front line employees were not as friendly as

they should be. He was in the habit of popping into his hotels unannounced and prowling around fault finding often with a scowl on his face. His answer came one day from a page boy who said to him 'why don't *you* ever smile, Sir?' You cannot delegate the responsibility to model behaviour: wherever you sit on the organizational ladder you must do your own behaviour modelling and you should be aware that the benefits of correct behaviour modelling of supervisors and departmental managers can be seriously affected if the man at the top does not display the correct behaviour.

Same sex and race as the observer; is apparently friendly and helpful
We cannot, of course, change our sex or race but it is an interesting point to bear in mind when making management appointments. We can all, of course, try to be friendly and helpful.

When the trainee is rewarded for engaging in the depicted behaviour
The trainee or employee can and should be rewarded at minimum with praise from the employer, but often far greater reward will come by the reaction of the hotel guest to the hotel employee. An employee who begins to practice behaviour designed to please the guest and to satisfy the guest's needs will soon experience the rewards as the guest becomes more friendly, more relaxed and possibly even leaves bigger monetary tips.

When the modelling display depicts behaviour to be modelled in a vivid and detailed manner
Successful hotelkeeping is all about details. As mentioned earlier there is no exceptionally complicated process in hotelkeeping. The difficult thing is combining all the tiny details into one complete enterprise, but, first of all, attention must be given to details for it is just these details that are important and the sum total of correct details will result in the perfect whole. For example, ashtrays in lobbies must be kept clean, maids must clean under soap dishes in bathrooms, curtain hooks must be all attached in restaurants, music must be played at the right sound levels, etc. Whilst managers are demonstrating behaviour as 'models' therefore it is absolutely essential that they do it in detail. Vague references to what must be done are useless; you must actually pick up the litter!

In order from least to most difficult behaviour
This can only really be achieved effectively in the classroom because in the real world you cannot select which order the tasks will appear. You can, of course, make sure that employees are correctly settled into jobs

which match their capabilities or at least are only one rung above to stretch them.

With sufficient frequency and repetitiveness
This is vital and this is why *being there* as a manager is important. Unless you, as manager, are where the action is you will not be able to observe your employees in their real life 'role plays' and will not be able to give them continuous feedback. Nor will you be able to understand the difficulties they are faced with and the excuses they therefore may come up with to alleviate potential poor behaviour. Organizational problems can get in the way. If you are there you can remove these obstructions and if you are there frequently you can give frequent feedback until employee behaviour is improved to a point where rewards are obtained and 'pride in the job' is achieved. *Being there*, producing the model behaviour, observing the imitator and giving frequent feedback can only result in success.

With a minimum of irrelevant detail and when several different models rather than a single model are utilized
In hotels several different models have to be utilized because by the nature of a twenty-four hour business no one model manager can be everywhere around the clock and the organization is normally so structured that managers, assistant managers and department supervisors work in shifts. If all of them display correct modelling behaviour the overwhelming nature of the modelling available must surely affect the behaviour of the employee?

One of the greatest examples of behaviour modelling that I have witnessed and been involved in took place on the island of Mauritius in the Indian Ocean. My company had decided to build a resort hotel there on a beautiful beach peninsular. During the planning and construction stage of the hotel we had cause to stay in most of the other existing hotels on the island and we became increasingly alarmed at what appeared to be the poor level of employees available and at their surliness and unhelpful nature.

However, we were frequently at these hotels at dinner times (since we were working through the day) and were, therefore, able to observe what we thought to be the root of the problem. Management was never in evidence until the height of the dinner service when the manager would ceremoniously arrive and, looking straight ahead, would be escorted to the best table, whereupon three or four waiters would serve him irrespective of the chaos reigning around him. You could feel the tremors of resentment against him amongst the staff. The same type of behaviour was exhibited in all of the hotels we visited.

We, therefore, decided that it was essential for us to behave as model managers in all we did with regard to our own new project and this is exactly what happened. Even before the hotel opened we demonstrated to our newly hired employees that we could work twice as hard and long as they could, that we could carry just as many chairs and tables as they could, clean up the builder's mess just as well as they could, and so on. When the hotel opened we made sure that every guest was met politely and sincerely, that we called them by their names, that we never ate until the peak had passed and so on.

Within weeks our staff and the service they provided at the St. Geran Hotel had become the talk of the island and not long after the talk of the resort hotel world. The hotel was instantly successful, mainly due to the warmth and friendliness of the employees – on an island where all other employees seemed to have been unhappy!

6 *Please Tell me Why?*

Other conditions than having merely excellent 'model' managers must exist, of course, to achieve excellent 'performance' from hotel employees. The necessity for employees to be highly motivated and fully responsible is obvious in most enterprises but the hotel industry, much like the retail industry, places a higher burden on the shoulders of its employees than most other businesses do. The similarity between the hotel industry and the retail industry is striking and hotel management students could find it interesting to read *People Productivity in Retailing* (Friedland, Israel and Lynch, 1980). Both industries rely extremely heavily on the performance of their 'front line' personnel who in both instances form by far the bulk of all people employed in the enterprise. The skill, efficiency, pleasantness and mood of each of these employees is vital to the success of the enterprise. A guest can stay in an hotel for three days, be wonderfully treated by all the staff, but upon leaving may be discourteously treated by one. That 'one' can ruin the good work of all the others. In the introduction *People Productivity in Retailing* the authors state the following: 'Competing retailers often have the same access to markets, to customers, and technology. It is how they develop their people that makes the difference. *People do make the difference.* They can be developed into productive employees who will give you the edge over your competitors'.

People, i.e. the employees, also make the difference in the hotel industry, but there are some dissimilarities between the two industries which make the performance of individual hotel employees even more crucially important to the success of the enterprise than their retailing counterparts. Two factors give the hotel industry a sort of uniqueness.

The first is the fact that the hotel industry in concerned with service and production at the same time. Retailing is only concerned with service or the sale of goods. In many instances, particularly in the restaurant side of the industry, the goods are both manufactured and retailed in the same time frame so not only is there a burden on the performance of the serving personnel but stresses are also created between these personnel and those concerned with the 'production'. The effect and control of these stresses is examined in the next chapter. The uniqueness of the situation however is that if there is a delay in production the customer is *immediately* affected.

The second factor is that of time. An hotel offers a product and service *today*. If it does not sell that product or service today it can never ever sell it today again. This is particularly true of room sales for an empty room on one night is lost revenue for ever and ever, but even in restaurants non sales can result in costly waste.

All of this places a tremendous burden on the shoulders of hotel employees if they are to perform satisfactorily. The wrong answer to a phone call can cost a room night, not answering a phone in time can do likewise, a slow kitchen may cost you a customer, etc., etc.

For a hotel to function well, therefore, its staff must be not only technically and behaviourally well trained but they must be highly motivated. How can their relationship with management and the style of management work towards creating such levels of high motivation and commitment?

The first thing that we have already touched upon is communication. As mentioned in the discussion on communication between manager and guest, good communication between manager and employee is fundamentally required and by *being there* with his employees under pressure the manager will be placing himself in a position to communicate. But what should he communicate and how?

There can be no doubt that sharing information with employees is one of the keys to motivation. Since one is so utterly reliant on their performance in the face of the customer and since one has given them the responsibility of representing the business to the customer then one should feel they are 'responsible' enough to receive and assimilate information about the state and affairs of the business. People like to be involved and as a general rule the more information one can pass down the more it is appreciated and the more the employees feel a part of the enterprise they are being asked to represent. The following figure is a useful tool to analyse the depth of information which you wish to impart.

```
        Could know

      Should
       know

      Must
      know
```

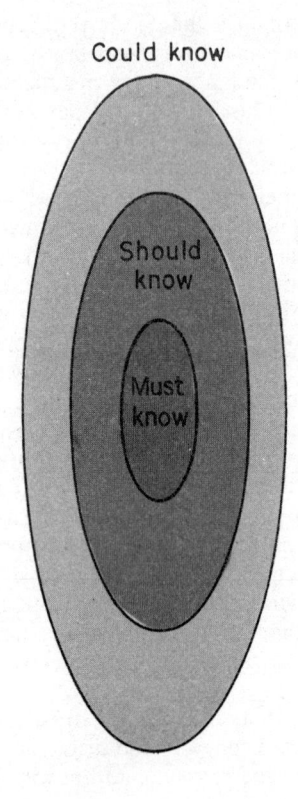

There is much information which an employee *must* know in order to do his job properly. For example he must know what hours he is expected to work, where he gets his uniform, who is his boss, what are the rules of his department, etc. There are other things that he *should* know. For example, if he is a hall porter he should know the layout of the hotel, the opening times of the restaurants, the location of other hotels in the chain, etc., etc. And then there are things which he *could* know which may be useful in the direct performance of the job but may be more in the nature of making him feel involved and part of the 'family' which is the enterprise. For example, the name of the chief executive of the company, the current occupancy of the hotel compared with last year, the number of covers being served in the restaurants or 'How am I doing in the job', etc., etc.

Many, many hotels do an exceptionally poor job of passing on to their employees even the information that they must know as can be witnessed by the number of hotel employees around who do not appear to know what they are supposed to be doing. Much of this communication is, of course, pure training but it should start with job induction. Unfortunately one so often hears 'Who has got time for that? We've got to get on with the job'. All hotel employees should be properly inducted because if it is not done before they 'get on with the job' one can never get hold of them to do it once they have started. And after all, if one did not have them yesterday to do the job one can probably get by without them today – the day that they get their induction. The most practical approach to induction in an hotel is to sort out what one wishes to tell each starting employee into 'must know', 'should know', and 'could know' information. The 'must know', category probably relates very heavily to his particular job or department and he cannot start unless he gets this information. It is therefore practicable for this to be given to him on day one by his department head, following (hopefully) a preplanned, prewritten check list. Once a week the new 'starters' from all departments can be gathered together 'off the job' and given a presentation by somebody who has been trained to do so, in the 'should knows' and even the 'could knows' of the organization. The imparting of a few 'could knows' to newcomers always creates an impressive start. For example it is unnecessary for a dishwasher to know what the hotel penthouse looks like whereas it is necessary for a front desk clerk to know. Why not, however, include the dishwasher in the tour of the front of house facilities? He will go home that night and relate his impressions of where he works with pride.

Many hotel executives are very nervous of sharing financial information with employees. I have never been nervous and have always shared as much as I had time to or I believed the receiver could assimilate. Obviously different categories of employee will be interested in or be able to assimilate and understand varying degrees of information. The distribution and discussion of operating information and statistics has always in my experience been received with interest and enthusiasm by my employees and to my knowledge has never been abused. 'Don't tell them that' I have often been told by fellow directors, 'They will leak it to our opposition!' 'So what?' is my normal retort. Of course, some information must be classified because its general release could be harmful to the operation. The nature of this information however is generally so specific, e.g. information on takeover bids, acquisitions, sales of property, personnel changes, etc. that its very nature clearly 'red flags' it as information that no one would expect to be passed down. Having made the personnel change or acquisition however one must remember to tell the personnel before one tells the world!

Remember always that the manner in which one communicates to the employees is important, be it in a formal meeting, large or small, or whilst *being there* with your employees. In the process of communication bear in mind the following subtle differences of style.

EVALUATION versus DESCRIPTION

When giving 'feedback' or information to an employee on his performance try to be descriptive rather than evaluative. If one simply describes the action of the employee and the result of that action in an objective fashion without trying to place a value of right or wrong on the action one stands a chance of being listened to. If one commences by an evaluative statement it will be met by a 'defensive' mind.

CONTROL versus INFORMATION

Try to communicate by giving information that will help solve problems rather than giving information that will be perceived to be 'controlling'. People react positively to a supply of information, statistics, data that highlight problems to be solved rather than information which they perceive as being produced to control them.

STRATEGY versus SPONTANEITY

Be spontaneous and open. Don't appear to be devious or involved in strategy in your communications. Be straightforward. People distrust 'strategy'.

NEUTRALITY versus POSITIVENESS

Be firm and positive (although leave room for change sparked by contribution from the employees to whom one is communicating). Do not be neutral and wishywashy. People do not go for leaders who sit on the fence. Someday these same employees will be looking for support and they will not expect to get it from a fence-sitter.

SUPERIORITY versus EQUALITY

Do not come across as a superior human being. One does not have to defend one's own self image. Come across as an equal *human being* doing a different job and wearing a different hat to the person you are addressing. People stick pins into people who blow themselves up as self-important balloons.

The time that one chooses to communicate is, of course, dependant upon the type and urgency of the information. An analysis of the communication network in the hotel should be made. Plan to handle each type of communication in the most effective manner. Consider:

What items are to be communicated?
Who is the best person to handle the communication and from whom will the listeners receive it best?
To whom should it be communicated?
Through what medium?
What effect do you expect to achieve by the communication?

Finally, remeber one golden rule. When telling someone to do something, tell them why!

7   The Crucial Relationship – Manager to Employee

It is obvious that managers must communicate. The reader may, however, be asking at this stage whether my preference for sharing as much information as possible is based on purely my own good experiences of this style or whether it stems from a deeper and more researched study of others' experiences as well. Voluminous research and writing has been performed on this subject which in turn forms part of a far bigger subject, i.e. the relationship of boss to subordinate.

The fundamental debate that has raged in most industries and in most writings on this subject has been on the question of just how participative or just how authoritative management style should be. No specific research has taken place in the hotel industry although during the fifties and sixties much was written on the subject of 'participative' versus 'authoritative' management. The reader is thoroughly recommended to read *The Human Side of Enterprise* by the late Douglas McGregor, a book which had massive impact on management style following its publication in 1960. McGregor studied the attitudes of supervisors and managers and identified two sets of attitudes which are frequently found. One he called Theory X, the other Theory Y. It would seem that most supervisors operate under either Theory X or Theory Y.

The two theories, as described by Douglas McGregor, are as follows.

Theory X

1 Management is responsible for organizing the elements of

productive enterprise – money, materials, equipment, people – in the interest of economic ends.
2. With respect to people, this is a process of directing their efforts, motivating them, controlling their actions, modifying their behaviour to fit the needs of the organization.
3. Without this active intervention by management, people would be passive – even resistant – to organizational needs. They must therefore be persuaded, rewarded, punished and controlled – their activities must be directed. This is management's task – in managing subordinate managers or workers. We often sum it up by saying that management consists of getting things done through other people.

Behind this conventional theory there are several additional beliefs – less explicit, but widespread:

4. The average man is by nature indolent – he works as little as possible.
5. He lacks ambition, dislikes responsibility, prefers to be led.
6. He is inherently self-centred, indifferent to organizational needs.
7. He is by nature resistant to change.
8. He is gullible, not very bright, the ready dupe of the charlatan and the demagogue.

The human side of economic enterprise today is fashioned from propositions and beliefs such as these. Conventional organization structures, managerial policies, practices, and programs reflect these assumptions.

Theory Y

1. Management is responsible for organizing the elements of productive enterprise – money, materials, equipment, people – in the interest of economic ends.
2. People are not by nature passive or resistant to organizational needs. They have become so as a result of experience in organization.
3. The motivation, the potential for development, the capacity for assuming responsibility, the readiness to direct behaviour toward organizational goals are all present in people. Management does not put them there. It is a responsibility of management to make it possible for people to recognize and develop these human characteristics for themselves.

4 The essential task of management is to arrange organizational conditions and methods of operation so that people can achieve their own goals best by directing their own efforts toward organizational objectives.

This is a process primarily of creating opportunities, releasing potential, removing obstacles, encouraging growth, providing guidance. It is what Peter Drucker has called 'management by objectives' in contrast to 'management by control'.

I have personally always tried to manage more in accordance with the assumptions of Theory Y than those of Theory X and my experience seems to concur with much research which indicates that Theory Y assumptions about people's attitudes are closer to the truth. Theory Y, however, does not involve abdication of management, absence of leadership or the lowering of standards. It is not a 'soft' approach to management. It is, in fact, more difficult to achieve but potentially more successful.

Another approach to the analysis of management style was taken by Blake and Mouton in their original book *The Managerial Grid*. In this volume readers are able to observe the range of management behaviour depicted on a grid which has as its two axes 'concern for people' and 'concern for production'.

Blake and Mouton describe some managers as having high concern for production and low concern for people ('9.1' managers), others with high concern for people and low concern for production ('1.9' managers) and still others who exhibit concern for both ('9.9' managers). The reader will find this volume helpful in thinking through one's own 'style' and evaluating the results.

For the purposes of this book, however, the approach taken by Rensis Likert, Director of the Institute for Social Research at the University of Michigan has been reproduced in more detail.

Rensis Likert has broken down management behaviour in dealing with subordinates into four systems. A brief description of the systems as they relate to leadership processes follows.

Organizational variable	System 1	System 2	System 3	System 4
1 Leadership processes used				
Extent to which superiors have confidence and trust in subordinates.	Have no confidence and trust in subordinates	Have condescending confidence and trust, such as master has to servant	Substantial but not complete confidence and trust; still wishes to keep control of decisions	Complete confidence and trust in all matters
Extent to which superiors behave so that subordinates feel free to discuss important things about their jobs with their immediate superior	Subordinates do not feel at all free to discuss things about the job with their superior	Subordinates do not feel very free to discuss things about the job with their superior	Subordinates feel rather free to discuss things about the job with their superior	Subordinates feel completely free to discuss things about the job with their superior
Extent to which immediate superior in solving job problems generally tries to get subordinates' ideas and opinions and make constructive use of them	Seldom gets ideas and opinions of subordinates in solving job problems	Sometimes gets ideas and opinions of subordinates in solving job problems	Usually gets ideas and opinions and usually tries to make constructive use of them	Always gets ideas and opinions and always tries to make constructive use of them
2 Character of motivational forces				
Manner in which motives are used	Fear, threats, punishment, and occasional rewards	Rewards and some actual or potential punishment	Rewards, occasional punishment, and some involvement	Economic rewards based on compensation system developed through participation; group participation and involvement in setting goals, improving methods, appraising progress toward goals, etc.

Organizational variable	System 1	System 2	System 3	System 4
Amount of responsibility felt by each member of organization for achieving organization's goals	High levels of management feel responsibility; lower levels feel less; rank and file feel little and often welcome opportunity to behave in ways to defeat organization's goals	Managerial personnel usually feel responsibility; rank and file usually feel relatively little responsibility for achieving organization's goals	Substantial proportion of personnel, especially at high levels, feel responsibility and generally behave in ways to achieve the organization's goals	Personnel at all levels feel real responsibility for organization's goals and behave in ways to implement them
3 Character of communication process				
Amount of interaction and communication aimed at achieving organization's goals	Very little	Little	Quite a bit	Much with both individuals and groups
Direction of information flow	Downward	Mostly downward	Down and up	Down, up and with peers
Extent to which downward communications are accepted by subordinates	Viewed with great suspicion	May or may not be viewed with suspicion	Often accepted but at times viewed with suspicion; may or may not be openly questioned	Generally accepted, but if not, openly and candidly questioned
Accuracy of upward communication via line	Tends to be inaccurate	Information that boss wants to hear flows; other information is restricted and filtered	Information that boss wants to hear flows; other information may be limited or cautiously given	Accurate

Psychological closeness of superiors to subordinates (i.e. how well does superior know and understand problems faced by subordinates?)	Has no knowledge or understanding of problems of subordinates	Has some knowledge and understanding of problems of subordinates	Knows and understands problems of subordinates quite well	Knows and understands problems of subordinates very well
4 Character of interaction – influence process				
Amount and character of interaction	Little interaction and always with fear and distrust	Little interaction and usually with some condescention by superiors; fear and caution by subordinates	Moderate interaction, often with fair amount of confidence and trust	Extensive, friendly interaction with high degree of confidence and trust
Amount of co-operative teamwork present	None	Relatively little	A moderate amount	Very substantial amount throughout the organization
5 Character of decision-making process				
At what level in organization are decisions formally made?	Bulk of decisions at top of organization	Policy at top, many decisions within prescribed framework made at lower levels	Broad policy and general decisions at top, more specific decisions at lower levels	Decision-making widely done throughout organization, although well integrated through linking process provided by overlapping groups

Organizational variable	System 1	System 2	System 3	System 4
To what extent are decision-makers aware of problems, particularly those at lower levels in the organization?	Often are unaware or only partially aware	Aware of some, unaware of others	Moderately aware of problems	Generally quite well aware of problems
Extent to which technical and professional knowledge is used in decision making	Used only if possessed at higher levels	Much of what is available in higher and middle levels is used	Much of what is available in higher, middle, and lower levels is used	Most of what is available anywhere within the organization is used
To what extent are subordinates involved in decisions related to their work?	Not at all	Never involved in decisions; occasionally consulted	Usually are consulted but ordinarily not involved in the decision making	Are involved fully in all decisions related to their work
Are decisions made at the best level in the organization so far as the motivational consequences (i.e. does the decision-making process help to create the necessary motivations in those persons who have to carry out the decisions?)	Decision making contributes little or nothing to the motivation to implement the decision, usually yields adverse motivation	Decision making contributes relatively little motivation	Some contribution by decision making to motivation to implement	Substantial contribution by decision making processes to motivation to implement

6 Character of goal setting or ordering				
Manner in which usually done	Orders issued	Orders issued, opportunity to comment may or may not exist	Goals are set or orders issued after discussion with subordinate(s) of problems and planned action	Except in emergencies goals are usually established by means of group participation
Are there forces to accept, resist, or reject goals?	Goals are overtly accepted but are covertly resisted strongly	Goals are overtly accepted but often covertly resisted, to, at least, a moderate degree	Goals are overtly accepted but at times with some covert resistance	Goals are fully accepted both overtly and covertly
7 Character of control process				
Extent to which the review and control functions are concentrated	Highly concentrated in top management	Relatively highly concentrated, with some delegated control to middle and lower levels	Moderate downward delegation of review and control processes; lower as well as higher levels feel responsible	Quite widespread responsibility for review and control, with lower units at times imposing more rigorous reviews and tighter controls than top management
Extent to which there is an informal organization present and supporting or opposing goals of formal organization	Informal organization present and opposing goals of formal organization	Informal organization usually present and partially resisting goals	Informal organization may be present and may either support or partially resist goals of formal organization	Informal and formal organization are one and the same, hence all social forces support efforts to achieve organization's goals

Organizational variable	System 1	System 2	System 3	System 4
Extent to which control data (e.g. accounting, productivity, cost, etc.) are used for self-guidance or group problem solving by managers and non-supervisory employees; or used by superiors in a punitive, policing manner	Used for policing and in punitive manner	Used for policing coupled with reward and punishment, sometimes punitively; used somewhat for guidance but in accord with orders	Largely used for policing with emphasis usually on reward but with some punishment; used for guidance in accord with orders; some use also for self-guidance	Used for self guidance and for co-ordinated problem solving and guidance; not used punitively

Likert's findings after immense research into many companies indicate that a manager employing System 4 is more likely to obtain high performance results for the organization than one using any of the other systems. That is because System 4 recognizes that the employee needs to maintain his sense of personal worth and importance.

McGregor's findings and also those of Blake and Mouton as well as many of their contemporaries seemed to concur with those of Likert. Also, in considering Maslow's human hierarchy of needs as it was examined in relation to guests' needs there is nothing to indicate that employees do not also have the same sets of needs – and what should make hotel employees any different from manufacturing or other service industry employees as far as fundamental human needs go?

To get the best out of one's employees it seems that the manager/employee relationship must be one which is supportive and ego-building. The manager's behaviour must be ego-building rather than ego-deflating; the manager must exercise enough empathy to see the problem or interaction in the light of the subordinate's expectations and background. In other words the manager must go out of his way to try to see things from the employee's point of view. Until he does so he can have no really effective communication with his subordinate. Such managerial behaviour is known as supportive.

In *The Human Organisation* Likert provided a list of questions to test supportive relationships. They are as follows.

1 How much confidence and trust do you feel your superior has in you? How much do you have in him?
2 To what extent does your boss convey to you a feeling of confidence that you can do your job successfully? Does he expect the 'impossible' and fully believe you can and will do it?
3 To what extent is he interested in helping you to achieve and maintain a good income?
4 To what extent does your superior try to understand your problems and do something about them?
5 How much is your superior really interested in helping you with your personal and family problems?
6 How much help do you get from your superior in doing your work?
   (a) How much is he interested in training you and helping you learn better ways of doing your work?

(b) How much does he help you solve your problems constructively – not tell you the answer but help you think through your problems?
(c) To what extent does he see that you get the supplies, budget, equipment, etc., you need to do your job well?
7 To what extent is he interested in helping you get the training which will assist you in being promoted?
8 To what extent does your superior try to keep you informed about matters related to your job?
9 How fully does your superior share information with you about the company, its financial condition, earnings, etc., or does he keep such information to himself?
10 Does your superior ask your opinion when a problem comes up which involves your work? Does he value your ideas and seek them and endeavour to use them?
11 Is he friendly and easily approached?
12 To what extent is your superior generous in the credit and recognition given to others for the accomplishments and contributions rather than seeking to claim all the credit himself?

In my experience almost every one of those questions could be asked of any hotel employee in almost any environment and at almost any level in the organization and if the answers were negative the hotel would not be functioning as well as it could.

The creation of a supportive environment should not be confused with the abdication of control or the removal of discipline. In no way is it suggested that management should absolve itself from these things.

In fact discipline is exceptionally important in achieving high standards but discipline invariably means confrontation and confrontation can be coped with within a supportive environment because people can call a spade a spade without fear of being misunderstood.

The larger the shaded areas of the Johari window (*see* Chapter 4) between manager and employee the better chance there will be of resolving misunderstandings and pushing for higher standards without resentment.

Furthermore, the opportunity for the manager to be supportive fits exactly into the *being there* style. Fortunately it is impossible for managers to have permanent meetings with all their employees because the guests do not organize their arrivals, departures or requests to fit in with the manager's meeting schedule. For a manager to make contact with his staff he must go to where they are doing the job and it is right there, on their own ground, that they will feel most comfortable in explaining their problems, in recommending new methods or systems, or in passing on guest feedback to the manager. Employees 'share' much more easily in their work environment than they do around a conference table!

A word of caution at this point. The reader should not assume that Likert's system 4 or McGregor's participative recommendations or my 'communicate all' approach are the only style of management – employee relationship for every occasion. As managers you will be required to assess the level of preparedness or maturity of your employees in order to plan your approach. Whichever style you choose to adopt as a manager you must, of course, bear in mind the nature of the persons you are managing. Your employees' behaviour will be a function of many factors including their hierarchy, their training and other environmental influences they have been subject to (including previous good and bad 'model' managers), their perceptions and their needs.

I had a startling demonstration of this when I first went to Africa. I had recently been handling strike negotiations in Milan for the Sonesta Hotel whose workers had 'struck' during the Milan October trade fair. The experience of Milan union negotiations was probably unparalleled (since the union called a strike at least every year) and therefore the negotiations were rather sophisticated. A few weeks later I was in South Africa being confronted with a strike of Zulu workers at the 450-room Elangeni Hotel in Durban. I flew to Durban and went through the usual process of trying to get the workers committee to come forward for discussions. After some time the hotel manager and I persuaded the committee to come inside for a meeting and we started what turned out to be a painfully slow process of trying to get to the root of the workers' complaints. After an hour or two my boss, the managing director of the company, telephoned from Johannesburg to ask how I was handling the situation. I explained I was holding an exploratory meeting. 'That's no use' he exclaimed, 'You've got to *tell* these Zulus what to do – not debate with them. I'm coming down!' Whereupon he rushed to the airport and joined me about three hours later, whilst the strike, of course, was still in progress. 'Follow me!' he said and we stomped to the loading bay at the back of the hotel where he climbed on a box and started shouting instructions to the crowd of strikers milling around the back door. 'Anyone who doesn't come back into the building before I count ten will be fired and will never work here again. When you're all back at work we'll listen to your grievances. One, two, three, etc.' By the count of three there was a trickle of movement towards the staff door, by ten there was a stampede. These Zulus were used to being 'told' what to do – not only by their bosses but by the tribal chiefs. They were just not prepared for or able to handle any consultative approach.

Before leaving this chapter on the manager and the employee a brief word on one of the results of motivated employees. In my experience motivated employees have been satisfied employees. One reason for this is that motivated employees provide a high level of service for which they are inevitably thanked by appreciative guests. It is from this appreciation that we can all get our 'kicks' in the hotel business. As a corporate executive of hotel companies for many years, often receiving only the letters of complaint, I sometimes began to wonder what it was all about – why was I doing all this? On several occasions I stepped in to run or assist in running hotels that were under severe pressure. Life became really worthwhile again when guests used to approach me as they settled their hefty accounts and said 'Thank you for all you have done for us. We really enjoyed our vacation'.

Let us return again to the findings of Frederick Herzberg whose research, as described in Chapter 2 was primarily concerned with this area of job satisfaction. Herzberg concluded that if you take the list of items below only a few of them are the cause of job satisfaction. See if you can pick out the 'satisfiers' from the list below:

1 Good pay or a salary increase.
2 The achievement on completing an important task successfully.
3 Good technical supervision.
4 Recognition or being singled out for praise.
5 Excellent company policies and administration.
6 Being given responsibility for one's own or others work.
7 Good working conditions and physical surroundings.
8 Advancement or changing status through promotion.
9 Job security.

The satisfiers are, in fact, all of the items with the even numbers. The difference is that if one is in employment where all of the odd-numbered conditions exist one does not get satisfied – one is merely not dissatisfied!

In other words if all of the odd-numbered conditions are removed one will become dissatisfied. When any or all of them are rectified one will not become satisfied, one will just cease to be dissatisfied. One will only become satisfied with the job if any or all of the even-numbered conditions exist.

You may be surprised to see that pay or a salary increase are not

The Crucial Relationship – Manager to Employee 67

satisfiers. Herzberg likens this to food. 'You eat, you get hungry, you eat again. You get paid, you work, you get paid again. If you don't get paid you get pretty unhappy. And if you have an increase, you are sure going to expect an increase again in the future. If you feel happy about an increase it will be because it is more than other people got – in other words your performance has been recognized. It is the recognition that satisfies you – not the salary increase.

Over a period of several years I have asked dozens of groups of hotel employees to write down one instance in their working lives that gave them a great feeling of satisfaction and one that dissatisfied them greatly. In every single case the satisfiers and dissatisfiers turned out to be exactly as Herzberg described.

The importance, therefore, of harnessing the human desire to achieve, to accept responsibility and to gain advancement, by creating a direction in the form of goals which stretch and interest the individual is critical to the success of managers. Getting them to mould their individual ambition in to an integrated team effort is the next problem.

8 *Interfaces and Openings*

We have spent considerable time in this book so far looking at management to guest relationships and management to employee relationships. Let us look now for a moment at the employees' relationship with each other, because in the same way that the guest will suffer if the employee feels resentful of the boss, the guest will suffer if the employee feels resentful of the boss, the guest can be in real trouble if the employees are not hitting it off with each other – and hotel organizations are designed so that they won't.

When I was a young 'commis' waiter in a large and famous hotel restaurant in London it struck me forcibly that the restaurant team and the kitchen team seemed to be engaged in a permanent battle rather than be working together for a common goal – to satisfy the guest.

I remember clearly the time when one of my 'tables' had ordered a desert flambé at the time of placing their main course order. In my eagerness to please the guests I had been observing their progress during the main course and at a certain point I went off to the kitchen to tell the chef to 'put the souffle on'. 'I'll get the bloody souffle ready when I bloody well like' was the retort. 'I'm in charge out here!' Needless to say the guests had a lengthy and unnecessary wait between main course and dessert which could have been avoided with a little team work.

The problem, of course, is an interesting organizational one because the interface between restaurant and kitchen in a traditionally organized hotel is one which does not work – and there are similar organizational interfaces across the hotel which also do not work. In the case of the restaurant and kitchen, one has the situation where the most junior inexperienced employee in the restaurant is sent to the kitchen with an 'order' to give to the most senior experienced chef and the process gets repeated over and over again throughout the meal (battle) period. The experienced chef often takes out his feelings on his work force and unnecessary traumas occur daily. How often can one observe great food preparation being spoiled on hotplates and in bainmaries due to lack of co-ordination between the kitchen and restaurant?

Consider for a moment the interface between the reception clerk and the housekeeping department. An arriving guest needs to be housed in room 622 which is shown on the 'board' as being vacated but not yet ready. The housekeeper has decided to get the seventh floor ready first and has given instructions to staff accordingly. Now here comes a 'junior' desk clerk *telling* her that he wants room 622 *now*. Suddenly it does not become the guest that needs the room; it is a 'jumped up' desk clerk who is just making things difficult for an experienced and mature supervisor. This type of difficult interface occurs time and time again throughout the industry and in each case, it is the paying guest who suffers.

Not only is the problem one of individual egos that get in the way of doing the job but the very nature of the organization of the jobs themselves. The hotel is made up of a series of working cells that are independent in the nature of their work but interdependent on each other for the creation of the overall product and service. Work is, however, generally conducted in 'cells' and therefore teams are built in each 'cell' and not in the overall. Cooks work in kitchens, waiters in restaurants, maids in bedrooms, clerks in offices, etc. The nature of their jobs keeps them apart and the nature of the work means that different types and different nationalities specialize in different departments. It is at the point of interface between the 'cells' that the flashpoints occur and since there is no waiting time between the customer giving the order and expecting it to be met, (not like the manufacturing business!) any breakdown at a flashpoint gets immediately transferred to the customer.

The trick that the hotel manager must pull off, therefore, is the achievement of an overall team, moulding together all the different components. It is interesting to observe, as I have done on many occasions, how the team building occurs, almost despite itself, during hotel opening situations. That is because most employees are very 'task' orientated, i.e. when there is a clearly definable goal, especially if the goal is of some magnitude, people do seem to settle their differences and pull together for the common good and the achievement of the goal. There can be no question for example that in the event of a nation being thrown into a war, provided that the people can identify with the purpose of the war, they will pull together in the most amazing way. Hotel openings can be the next worst thing to war! Dates are set when the doors will open, reservations are confirmed and things had just better be ready.

In these circumstances the staff, often thrown together from a variety of backgrounds, normally pull together incredibly well to achieve the task of opening the hotel. Problems start to occur soon after the opening. The task has been achieved; now what is the task? Merely satisfying the guests? People that just now were pulling together as a team now start to form groups and 'cells'. Poor morale and later poor service can easily set in. Inefficiencies and shortages that were overlooked at the time of opening for the common good are now highlighted and harped upon as reasons for poor service. Some practical ways by which this situation can be overcome and a team maintained are discussed in the ensuing chapters, but first let us take a closer look at what happens to management and employees during the pre-opening and opening period in a hotel's life.

I have personally been deeply involved in the pre-opening planning of over a dozen major hotels and the reader will forgive me, therefore, if I pass on some of my observations, with regard to 'operational' not 'construction' management of new ventures. The prime areas that a pre-opening 'operational' manager usually has to concern himself with are purchasing (operating equipment, uniforms, supplies, etc.), marketing, recruiting, training, operational and accounting systems design and the pre-opening book keeping and budgeting. He does not have to concern himself with guests nor the pressures of daily operations. He does have to have a clear programme working towards an 'opening' and must exercise enormous self discipline in the early stages in order not to be overcome with the volume of activities towards the end, as more and more uninitiated staff turn to him for help.

The operational opening of an hotel is a highly complex exercise involving careful planning and incredible attention to detail. In purchasing, for example, the manager must carefully evaluate the size, shape, style, quanitity, etc. of every single piece that is purchased, he must plan when it should arrive, where he will store it, how he will account for it, etc., etc. The level of planning and co-ordination skills required is far in excess of that required by management for ongoing operations.

A number of things are important to remember:

1 Do not plan or buy too early. One thing is certain in the planning of an hotel and that is that your plans will change and change again. As projects grow from paper plans to reality, things become apparent that could not easily be read from the plans. Restaurants somehow look smaller, restaurant chairs and tables seem bigger, the contractors hit rock and have to change the direction of the layout, the owners run out of money and cut back on an area, etc., etc. The later key purchasing decisions are taken the less waste there will eventually be.
2 Do not write voluminous manuals. American companies frequently spend massive sums of money preparing pre-opening operational manuals, which then have to be rewritten with every pre-opening change and are often put in a drawer and ignored once the hotel has opened and the 'real' events have overtaken the 'paper' ones. The time to write manuals in my view is after the hotel has been operating for six months. I will happily refund the price of this book to any reader who can show me a pre-opening operational manual of any type that was being faithfully followed six months after an 'opening'.
3 Do not hire staff too early. It is expensive and the task of managing people with not enough to do will overcome the task of planning the opening. Also contractors never complete areas of the building according to plan so the staff you hired to 'train' in the area will become an embarrassment and will loose 'steam' before the opening build up.
4 Concentrate on items which relate to the construction. Worry about systems and people and service once they are for real. Your priority before the opening should be to make sure that what the construction people are delivering to you works properly. If it does not function properly after the opening or if it is incorrectly built, you will really struggle to get it changed or amended – if you're lucky enough ever to see the builder again.
5 At the time of the opening do not just *be there* – *be everywhere*. The most intense role play you will ever have the chance to witness and to use as data for feedback will be happening all around you all the time. Remember that however carefully you have planned operations without guests, (even including

dummy runs) real guests have a habit of doing or wanting things you had not bargained for. You must make corrections fast.

6 Plan on at least one disaster. In some hotels it will be the plumbing, in others the air conditioning, in others the sewage, and, in one I was involved in, it was man-eating fish! You can count on it – something will go horribly wrong and you will have to have the staff behind you to cope with it. Which brings us back to the theme of this chapter – how *will* you get the staff behind you?

Up to and immediately after the opening this does not normally present a problem for the simple reason that the task or the goal is clear. Every single person who has been hired knows that he has been hired initially for the purpose of getting the hotel open. There are no 'guests' to worry about (who, after all, in the future will occupy the majority of most of the staff's time either directly or indirectly) and so new employees spend a lot of time doing such things as unpacking boxes, polishing silver, trying on uniforms, cleaning up – all activities which are clearly aimed at preparation for the big day of opening. To the most simple soul – the task is apparent. There is a deadline to meet and it has been clearly communicated to all concerned. The whole atmosphere is so charged with expectancy and hurly burly and rush that the entire team somehow pulls together to get the job done – irrespective often of the fashion in which it is accomplished.

The day of reckoning arrives, everyone is geared up and ready, the opening banquets are served and somehow everybody muddles through with often the experienced helping out the inexperienced.

And then? Nothing. A lull perhaps. The same old routine day after day. What is there to shoot for now? Items which prior to the opening were overlooked such as ice machines that do not work or blocked-up kitchen drains, now become a major issue and are 'somebody's fault. "We can't cook anything here until 'maintenance' fix the drains!" (Maintenance are probably busy finishing the contractor's work hanging closet doors in guest bedrooms.) Experienced workers get depressed with the inexperienced's failure to learn. Departmental groupings and 'cells' start to occur. Positions start to harden and suddenly the organizational monster has taken over – and many of the staff you have so carefully but expensively trained take off for pastures new, where the 'grass will be greener'. Have you ever noticed that the service in a new hotel is often better on day 1 than on day 101?

Two things have to be done. First, the employees must be given a new goal and secondly the 'cells' must be broken down. These problems are considered in Chapters 9 and 10.

9 Setting 'Goals'

Much has been written by many management and behavioural authors on the subject of 'setting goals' and students should familiarize themselves with the theory and practice of what is normally known as management-by-objectives (MBO).

Most MBO manuals concentrate on the processes of goal setting and achievement measurement and advise that a framework is required within which to catergorize objectives and thus make them more clearly identifiable and understandable by the employees. The framework that I have always found to be most understandable to hotel employees incorporates the following headings:

      financial goals;
      guest satisfaction goals;
      human resource goals;
      marketing goals.

Try to think about an hotel enterprise along the lines of the figure below which indicates clearly what major functions are to be carried out by an hotel manager.

Let us pause for a moment to analyse the figure on the following page.

Financial aspects
Relates to everything to do with all assets (excluding the human resource asset). It involves controls, accounting, pricing, payroll, cash management, control of the physical assets, etc.

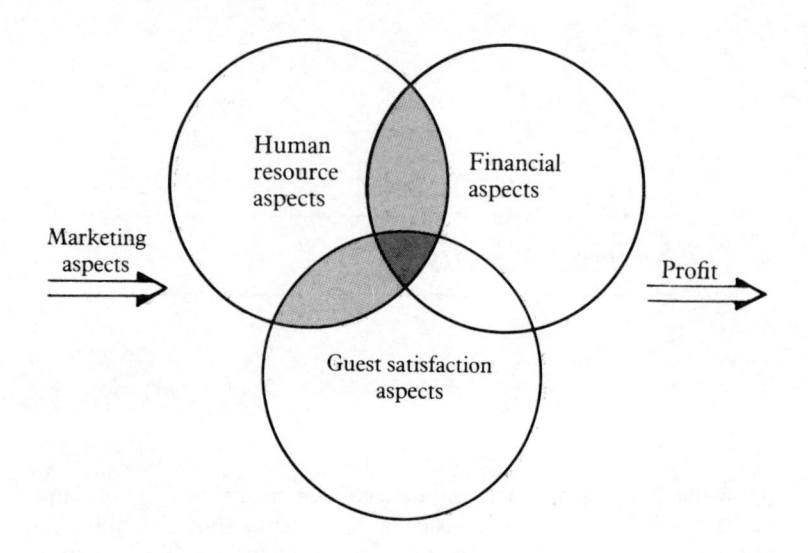

Human resource aspects
Relates to everything to do with employees, i.e. man management skills, hours of work, training, recruiting, employee morale, etc.

Guest satisfaction
Relates to satisfying existing clients, giving good service, value for money, standards of cuisine, standards of accommodation and maintenance, etc.

Marketing
Relates to getting more clients: advertising, Public relations, sales, etc.

If all of these activities are properly carried out and pieced together the enterprise will maximize its profits (or minimize its losses, if it was financially ill-conceived in the first place).

The first three aspects must stand together and are clearly the responsibility of the hotel manager. Marketing may or may not be within the scope of the manager's responsibility and, in my view, it invariably should not be if it can be accomplished by an independent sales team or person because:

1 The best marketing activity an hotel manager can indulge in is satisfying the needs of those guests who are already in the hotel. At least they know where it is, are likely to come back, and, if

happy, will tell their acquaintances about it. A really fine hotel should eventually require no marketing activity whatsoever save perhaps for an ongoing public relations effort.
2 Time spent by the manager on marketing means time not spent by the manager with his guests.
3 Marketing often means 'nice' things to hotel managers, like going on trips, going out to lunch, socializing at travel agents' cocktail parties and SKAL lunches – all of which are essential but not necessarily as essential as 'watching the store'.

The other activities of managing human resources, finance and guest satisfaction are all exceptionally interdependent and have to be properly orchestrated. If there is too much emphasis on one-third of the pie, profits will eventually suffer.

For example, if you pay staff too high a salary the human resource section will score well but the finance section will suffer and the business will go broke. If you pay 'correctly' both sections will survive. Similarly, if you charge too little for your rooms you may have guest satisfaction (in the value for money bracket) but your finance section will again come unstuck.

If you charge too much for your rooms in order to pay your staff too much you will, of course, have unhappy guests and happy staff – until you have no more guests – then everyone will be unhappy. All three are inextricably linked but are fortunately clearly definable. Without question the most important is guest satisfaction because without guests there will be nothing else, *but* guest's satisfaction must clearly be achieved whilst maintaining the equilibrium of the other sections of the chart or the result will be – no profit!

Never forget this simple diagram because it can be the basis of all overall operational analysis and hotel management effective self-analysis. At any one point in the life of an hotel you will be able to examine that hotel to see if the pie has the correct recipe because its ingredients need to be perfectly measured. In nearly all instances you will find that one-third of the diagram is scoring good marks to the detriment of one or two others. As a manager you must examine each section to see what corrective action needs to be taken.

In some hotels you will find 'fat and happy' staff, satisfied guests, and no profit. On examination you will see that there are too many staff and that you can still satisfy guests and even improve on their satisfaction with less employees. In another hotel you will find unhappy guests because portion control is too tight or because physical standards have been allowed to lapse. The business must be examined in each three sections and the impact of their interrelation with the other sections must be carefully considered. Having done this, improvement goals for the organization can be set, and set in such a way that they become meaningful things for employees to focus on and understand.

My basic recommendations for setting improvement goals are as follows:

1. Involve your supervisors in suggesting goals and get your supervisors to involve their workers. To do this you will have to share certain financial information with your supervisors. Structure the information in simple terms.
2. Analyse your clients' reaction to your services – by ongoing personal observation, guest comment forms, and guest history information.
3. Compare your performance with similar operations – either by using Laventhol & Horwath or Harris Kerr Foster's annual hotel trends reports or with information from sister company hotels.
4. Do not have too many goals. Between seven and ten in my experience is an ideal number that can be concentrated on and followed up.
5. Make sure that there is a spread of goals across all three sections of the chart, although concentrate on the weakest segment.
6. Make the goals measurable and specific. i.e. reduction in guest complaints, increase in repeat reservations, speeding up of breakfast service, increasing restaurant covers, etc.
7. Communicate the goals clearly to your supervisors and assist them in getting their employees to understand them by continually seeing their involvement and feeding back on progress.
8. Review progress periodically and reset goals. Do not let the goals drop out of sight. They are 'living' items. As one of the goals is neared bring in another one.
9. Keep it simple. Do not overburden the whole process with too much paperwork or you'll kill it.
10. Make sure the goals are 'stretching', i.e. not too easily attainable but within reach.

This ongoing process of setting and reviewing targets will give you and your organization a sense of purpose and direction which it otherwise might lack. It will create opportunities for employees to self measure and to be spurred on to greater achievement.

After many experiments with university students who were set specific tasks to achieve in 'laboratory controlled' conditions Locke (Locke, Cartledge and Knerr, 1970) concluded the following: "Specific performance goals (above a certain critical magnitude) elicit higher performance on tasks than do instructions to 'do your best', and in general the more difficult the performance goal (so long as it is accepted by the individual) the higher the performance".

10 *An Hotel Needs a Team*

Once familiar with your own brew of MBO you will find that supervisors and employees naturally pick out, work upon and become interested in the objectives which directly affect them to the exclusion and the positive disinterest in objectives which relate to other departments of the hotel. A side effect of MBO can, therefore, be to build teams in 'cells' but deepen the gorge between the 'cells'. How then can the cells be broken down?

Hotels, as we have seen, are organized departmentally and the following organization chart, although oversimplified, is probably not untypical.

Each supervisor and employee fits into his or her own little box and is expected to perform activities commensurate with the requirements of the box. Each person is given a title and learns to play to a known set of rules. What then begins to happen is a rather strange phenomenon – the titles and the uniform of the person start to dictate that persons' behaviour more than their personalities do. An executive chef begins behaving in a manner which he thinks is appropriate for an executive chef which may be completely different from how he behaved as a sous chef or a commis chef even though he is still the same personality. A head housekeeper will behave in a manner which she has perceived to be correct behaviour for a head housekeeper which again may be a far cry from her behaviour as a floor supervisor.

Obviously some different forms of behaviour are required as one moves from position to position or is promoted. It is just not possible to be 'one of the girls' as a head housekeeper and at the same time maintain discipline. Behavioural changes however invariably are far

An Hotel Needs a Team 79

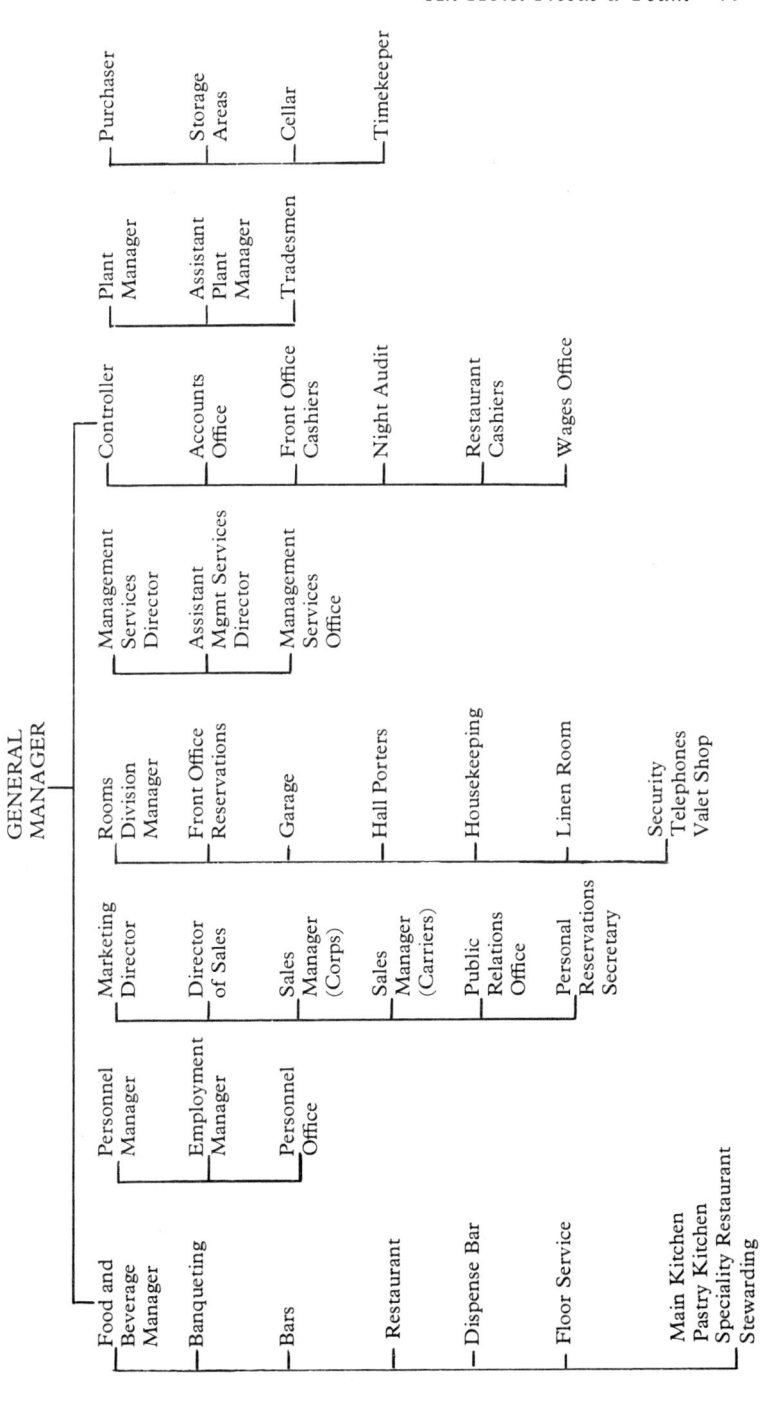

GENERAL MANAGER

Food and Beverage Manager
- Banqueting
- Bars
- Restaurant
- Dispense Bar
- Floor Service
- Main Kitchen
- Pastry Kitchen
- Speciality Restaurant
- Stewarding

Personnel Manager
- Employment Manager
- Personnel Office

Marketing Director
- Director of Sales
- Sales Manager (Corps)
- Sales Manager (Carriers)
- Public Relations Office
- Personal Reservations Secretary

Rooms Division Manager
- Front Office Reservations
- Garage
- Hall Porters
- Housekeeping
- Linen Room
- Security
- Telephones
- Valet Shop

Management Services Director
- Assistant Mgmt Services Director
- Management Services Office

Controller
- Accounts Office
- Front Office Cashiers
- Night Audit
- Restaurant Cashiers
- Wages Office

Plant Manager
- Assistant Plant Manager
- Tradesmen

Purchaser
- Storage Areas
- Cellar
- Timekeeper

greater than the mere change of position or 'box' dictates. They seem to be changes that are based on 'models' of stereotypes that fit the 'uniform'.

I remember spending a year in operational training at a luxury hotel in Park Lane, London, which in those days was one of the largest hotel organizations in existence. I very clearly felt that I was labelled a 'trainee' – not Peter Venison – human being. It seemed to me that everyone else behaved according to their 'uniforms' as well. The young fellows on the reception desk wore pinstripes and felt very self-important. The front office cashiers were older men but then they handled cash – you hardly dared to speak to them. The head concierge was 'God'. You practically needed an appointment to meet the chef. The whole place was like a theatre with people playing parts so often and so well that their real personalities had been completely lost and taken over by the required personality of the part.

This behaviour pattern is capable of dealing a death blow to team building and in hotel organizations frequently does. It is like trying to build a successful soccer team with all star players. In 1977 the New York Cosmos had some of the greatest individual soccer players in the world in their team including Pele, Santos, Beckenbaur, Chinaglia and so on. I once went to see them with high hopes of witnessing the greatest team in the history of soccer. They were awful – as a team – and Cosmos management shortly thereafter changed their policy of a 'star' system completely.

Hotel management, whilst retaining the 'stars' for public consumption (i.e. guest contact especially) just as Cosmos had to do to boost ticket sales, must somehow get employees to disregard their 'uniforms' and become human beings again when dealing with each other, because we have already seen what the self-esteem which goes with a uniform can do to co-operation at the various flash points or interfaces in the hotel organization.

In the mid-1960s I had the good fortune to initiate a programme of team development at the Carlton Tower Hotel in London which to my knowlege has never been repeated on such a scale in a single hotel. I was assisted and encouraged in this project by Jim Hynes, the then Director of Training for Hotel Corporation of America (now Vice President, Human Resources, Intercontinental Hotels), and shared the training responsibilities with Professor Philip Nailon of the University of Surrey and Geoff Pye now a Personnel Director at THF. To these gentlement I owe an enormous debt of gratitude for the exercise was not only stimulating but it proved to all that a planned approach to hotel team building can work.

For some years H.C.A. had been 'playing around' with sensitivity training – a form of training that was very popular in the 1960s that amongst other things attempted to change peoples' attitude in order that they would subsequently change their behaviour for their own good or in the case of industrial groups, for the good of their company.

The format of a 'T group' as sensitivity groups became called, was along the following lines. A group or groups of not more than twelve people and not less than eight would meet together for about six days in the same room or environment. There would be no set agenda but a 'trainer' and maybe an assistant trainer would be in attendance in the group. At the first and subsequent meetings with the group the trainers would do and say absolutely nothing thereby creating a complete 'vacuum' because the expectancies of all the participants would be for the trainers to start 'training' – as in all of the classroom experiences they had had before.

The resulting vacuum of course proves to be very uncomfortable for the participants who start to try to fill it, i.e. the brash ones will speak up and maybe express how foolish the whole thing is and 'why don't we all go to the bar?'; the thoughtful ones will restrain them by insisting that there must be a purpose to the whole thing so 'why don't we stick around and see what happens?'; the nervous ones will keep quiet. What they will all be doing is exhibiting behaviour and in most cases behaviour that they feel is expected of them or behaviour that is reminiscent of their back home 'uniforms', i.e. soldiers will tend to behave like soldiers, doctors like doctors, headwaiters like headwaiters, and so on.

As the process rolls on groupings begin to occur. Some people seem naturally attracted to others and seem naturally to dislike others. Feelings about others (because there is no other subject matter) begin to accumulate. The trainers have refused to accept the leadership role so they are rejected – cast aside. Other leaders develop; they are challenged and sometimes changed. Eventually the trainers, when enough behaviour has been displayed, start to ask reflective questions and get the group to concentrate on the behavioural processes that have been going on. They also guide the group into learning how to express their feelings about one another as one human being to another.

Slowly soldiers, doctors, and headwaiters disappear and real people emerge, expressing their feelings about themselves and their feelings for others – enlarging Johari's window. One by one participants learn to be truthful about themselves and as they do so (often a painful time) others step forward to help them through the difficult process. Participants ask for and receive feedback on their earlier behaviour and are told unhesitatingly by others how it affected the group. Participants get the chance to try out different forms of behaviour that are more acceptable to the group and continue to receive feedback. The participants learn to tolerate the fact that people are different. By the end of the week the group has grown through many stages of group life until it reaches interdependence – an understanding of others but a feeling of common bonds.

The assumptions underlying this form of training are as follows:

1 People can learn most effectively from an analysis of their own experience;
2 Feelings, attitudes and emotions are an essential ingredient of communication, but these are normally withheld;
3 In a suitably designed laboratory situation the forces against sharing feelings, attitudes and emotions can be overcome;
4 Individual members can learn how their own behaviour is perceived by others and gaining this information increases their insights about themselves;
5 Most of the forces to be overcome are essentially culturally acquired attitudes about what is a 'proper' form of social interaction.

(For a more detailed account of T groups students should read *T Group Theory and Laboratory Method*, by Bradford, Gibb and Benne, 1966).

H.C.A.'s President, Roger Sonnabend, had experienced such a group and immediately saw the benefits such training could have in building 'happy families' in his hotel company. His approach was to take some executives from the organization and send them to 'stranger' labs (i.e. lab for laboratory. The groups were regarded as human laboratories and 'stranger' because they were in groups of people from other companies and industries) in order to seed the organization with executives who understood the purpose and principles of such training. He then organized sessions which were attended by executives from different hotels in the H.C.A. group.

This, in my view, was a mistake, since although it benefited the participants as individuals and taught them plenty about group development and team building processes it did not build teams, because the participants came from all corners of the globe and would never have meaningful contact thereafter. (One thing it did do was to increase the intercompany hotel telephone accounts.) Furthermore when the participants returned to the 'back home' situation of their unit breathing 'love', 'goodwill', and other fine sentiments, their colleagues and subordinates often thought that they had gone off the rails.

It was at this point in the proceedings that I decided to adopt the principles involved in the programme (in which I had become deeply involved to the extent of being trained as a trainer) and adjust them to suit the needs of an individual hotel unit where team building was urgently required.

The Carlton Tower, although somewhat successful, had been run by a despot whose idea of team building was strictly 'divide and rule'. The despot passed away one day on the tennis court, and a fine new manager arrived with team building in his heart. The employees just were not used to a 'democratic' managerial approach since they were still divided. Together with the new manager the idea was conceived of taking them all, in groups, out of the work environment and submersing them into modified T group type sessions.

Approximately eighty persons were identified as supervisors from assistant managers down to third headwaiters and sous chefs. They were divided into eight groups of ten in diagonal slices across the organization. For example, a typical group of ten would be the rooms division manager, the head chef, the assistant steward, a floor housekeeper, a second head waiter, a reception chef de brigade, the head of payroll department, the concierge, a banquet salesman, the manager's secretary, and the F & B controller. In other words different types of employees from different levels of the organization.

A small hotel with about eight guest rooms was rented in the English countryside and eight team building programmes were run over an eleven week period with myself as resident trainer at all eight, assisted in some by Jim Hynes and in others by Philip Nailon and Geoff Pye.

The programme leant heavily on the T group style allowing long sessions each day and each evening for human laboratories but it was interspersed with lectures and exercises which primarily focused on communications and in particular homed in on problems within the Carlton Tower itself.

The results were spectacular. As the first group returned to the back home 'hostile' situation the second group had already left for the training programme. The first group held together as a team long enough for the second to return when the sharing of experiences suddenly bound both groups, with the third group already gone. By the end of seven or eight weeks it was the non-participants who felt out of the team and were 'eagerly' waiting their turns to be initiated.

The team spirit and co-operation which ensued the return of the final group was greater than I have witnessed in any other hotel environment. Several devices were used to keep up the momentum. Trios were formed with persons from different groups. They were asked to meet voluntarily once a month for a drink in the nearby pub to share views on the overall health of the team and to feed these into the Personnel Department. Several months after the initial programme a 'one-off' programme was run for people who had subsequently been promoted into supervisory positions or who had missed the first go-around for other reasons.

After about twenty months the momentum began to slacken and a second series of programmes was initiated with groups being put together on the same basis. The content of this programme was far more related to problem solving and goal setting at the Carlton Tower but did still include sizeable chunks of human 'lab' work. Momentum appeared to have been rekindled.

During the period of this work the profitability of the hotel increased dramatically, standards certainly improved since an atmosphere had been created where it was possible for management to confront problems without resentment, staff turnover was dramatically reduced, and, above all, employees seemed to enjoy coming to work. The benefits of guests meeting the same, mostly happy, faces were, of course, immeasurable.

A report was produced by Philip Nailon of the University of Surrey based on his experiences, and interviews of participants which were carried out by the 'Industrial Society'.

From this report entitled 'Organisation and Communication' the foreword is reproduced:

> 'Much is said about hotel operation being a 'people' business. That is to say that more than any other type of business, it is concerned with providing satisfactions for basic human needs – hunger and sleep. But through the interaction with staff other needs may be sought to be satisfied – security, acknowledgement and identity. The machinery for satisfying these needs is highly complicated and depends for its success on interactions between staff and staff and therefore on effective communication. Some elements of the customer's needs are unpredictable and what satisfies one may distress another. Hence communication must not only be accurate,

but it must also be speedy. Because accurate and speedy satisfaction of customer requirements often cuts across formal organizational departments, a need exists for effective communication between inter-related departments. For this to occur staff need to perceive and understand and be committed to the objectives of the enterprise. This implies free communication both upwards and downwards as well as sideways. For an enterprise to be successful, it needs to develop standards of performance through a system of staff appraisals. In dealing with finance and materials, standards are relatively easy to establish. But in defining standards of human performance considerable difficulty has been experienced. Only in an atmosphere of tust and openness can an appraisal system hope to be successful

'Most hotel and catering enterprises place emphasis on training in technical aspects of their work. Rarely is an attempt made to develop social skills and, of these, communication is more a topic for exhortation than practical training. At the same time it is appreciated that it is difficult to find a simple answer to the question 'How do you develop skill in communication?'. This report describes how one hotel tried to do this. It must be emphasized this is not a research study in the academic sense, but a descriptive account of a training programme and attempts to evaluate the results. It is hoped that in sharing this experience with those interested, by making this report available, it may help those whose thinking and philosophy are similar to the Carlton Tower.'

(The Carlton Tower was sold in 1970 and resold later in the decade. Notwithstanding this the hotel which was opened in 1960 still, in 1981, retains since opening, the same three headwaiters in the Rib Room, the same three headwaiters in the Chelsea Room, the same chef, pastry chef and several sous chefs, the same concierge and many others.)

Not all hotels require or can organize a team building effort on the scale of the one described above. The point is, however, that most hotel managements make no attempt to do anything at all in this area. Clearly there is much that can be achieved and not all team building programmes need be as involved as the one described. Professional help is available but it can be expensive. One would have to wonder what effects would occur if hotels took half of their marketing budgets each year and spent the money on team building. In many instances it could lessen the need for the other half of the marketing money altogether.

11 *Being There*

In Chapter 3 we looked at the reasons why it is important for an hotel manager to maximize his time on duty in the 'active' areas of the hotel. Hotel management, it seems, with the advance of hotel management training, has become more and more a 'nine to five' occupation filled with meetings, meetings and more meetings.

Guests, on the other hand do not synchronize their movements or actions to coincide with the 'nine to five' manager – in fact in commercial hotels, in particular, this is likely to be just the very period that they are out of the hotel attending to their own business. A duty of an hotel manager is clearly to analyse the nature of the particular enterprise and to plan management presence accordingly.

Needless to say it is impossible for a manager to be at the 'front' of his business twenty-four hours a day because there are many other duties he must perform. What he must do, therefore, is discipline himself, and his assistants, to be at the 'front' of the hotel when it counts most.

Whilst .interviewing hotelmen for managerial posts I have always asked them to describe a typical day in their life as a hotel manager. The results are astoundingly similar in as much that most hotel managers commence their day by going to the office to attend to the mail, from whence they emerge an hour or so later to go to the breakfast room – after all the action is over.

The prime meal in a commercial hotel is not lunch, nor dinner, but breakfast. In many business hotels the restaurant population for lunch and dinner is made up of visitors and hotel guests with very often the visitors outnumbering the hotel guests. At breakfast time the breakfast room is practically exclusively used by persons who have bought bedrooms the night before and, in the final analysis in most hotels, it is these people that are making the hotel profitable because the potential profit from 'rooms' business is far greater than from food and beverage.

Why not then concentrate on the movements of the hotel residents and analyse their high density areas in order to *be there*?

First, let us examine a good quality city centre hotel with a clientele of businessmen and tourists but a preponderance of businessmen. The first thing to do is to analyse the client mix. In so doing you will probably find that businessmen are dominant Sunday evening through Thursday and, if your marketing department is functioning well, tourists are dominant on Friday and Saturday through Sunday morning. The individual businessman is probably paying more per night than the tourist, but then the tourist could well be sent by a wholesaler who can send much repeat business, so both are important to the health of your enterprise. Indeed, it is safe to assume that all guests are important and get that message across to the staff. (Hotel employees have an uncanny way of knowing which guests are 'worthwhile' doing things for and which are on a budget, so it is particularly important that the 'model' manager displays the correct behaviour to tourists and, in particular, to tour leaders!).

A simple analysis of the guests' habits will show that, in general, businessmen are active earlier in the morning than tourists, that businessmen nearly all take breakfast in the hotel (and even invite guests to breakfast), and that businessmen are often looking to relax in the evening when many of them are at a loose end. With tourists who are travelling in groups – and the bulk do – their movements are easily identified through a briefing session with the tour leader.

The situation will, of course, be different from hotel to hotel but you will find it a fairly easy task to pin down the bulk movements of people in your own property.

Having done so, organize management time accordingly. Make sure that management – not just 'restaurant' management – are in the breakfast room every morning during peak periods. About half of your paying guests will be there too! This is a magnificent opportunity to meet your guests briefly but sincerely. They are certain to be in a bit of a hurry and will not want you to linger in small talk or to buy them a drink. You should move from table to table and introduce yourself to everybody and sincerely enquire if they are being well treated. If they are not, or if things have gone wrong during their stay, this early morning act of opening up a new section of your Johari window will give them every opportunity to tell you about their problems in a concise way. And remember, far better that they tell you at this point than the person they are going to meet in the office in an hour's time, because one sure thing is that they will tell somebody. You, Mr Manager, are the ideal person for them to unload upon because, first, you can take action to see that the same fate does not befall another guest and, secondly, you lessen greatly the risk of them telling an outsider – particularly if you demonstrate real concern and then fix the problem. (One way to demonstrate concern is to take a notepad with you for these jaunts to the breakfast room and be seen to be writing down the details.)

Do not do what I have observed most managers and assistant managers do at breakfast time, i.e. stick your head through the door, ask the maitre d'hotel if everything is all right, and withdraw it to the safety of the office. This is not *being there*! Try to choose the busiest half hour of the service and there is a good chance that you will meet up to twenty per cent of your entire guests in one sweep. Do not be afraid to take action where you see the service is slipping and furthermore do not be afraid to enter into the service yourself for not only is the guest impressed if he sees a manager clear a place or get a table ready and seat a guest, but so are the employees. Remember that if you just stick your head into the restaurant to ask the maitre d' if things are going well he will tell you they are – even if they are not. If he knows you can be of genuine help he will certainly welcome your presence.

What are the other pressure points in the early morning? Try room service and front desk cashiering. How do you maintain their efficiency? – by *being there*. Room service is at breakfast time absolutely linked to the dining room breakfast service e.g. if there are one hundred breakfast eaters in an hotel on one day twenty of them may eat in the dining room and eighty in their hotel rooms or another day exactly the reverse. You will, of course, maintain statistics to help staff the areas correctly but often the swing is inexplicable. If you are there however, at the right time, there are enough signals to indicate impending volumes (not least the bedroom door order form) and you, as manager, can easily overrule any interdepartmental flashpoint interface situation and swing waiters from restaurant to room service or vice versa as the situation demands. By *being there* you also have the chance to spot check quality and correctness of orders (i.e. to model correct behaviour) but you can only do this if you *stay there* for a while.

Of all the early morning stops a manager should make, the front desk cashiers can be the most illuminating – for it is here that he can really find out whether the guest enjoyed his or her stay. There can be no doubt that the hotel employee who receives the most feedback (good and bad) from guests is the person who renders the account. The account, of course, itemizes all of the guests' experiences of the last few days and serves to remind him of what went well and particularly of what did not. 'My God, $90 is a lot to pay for a room where the shower doesn't work!' or 'You've got a real nerve charging me for this breakfast – eventually I had to go out before it arrived!' or 'I never made all those telephone calls!' etc., etc. A manager on hand at this point can learn more about his hotel than he can anywhere else or any time else – and if he is prepared to step in and introduce himself to the complaining customer he can win many a repeat guest and prevent the bad word reaching the potential guests.

As a routine in this type of city hotel it is particularly important to come to work early and to have accomplished at least half an hour in the breakfast room, half an hour at the room service, and half an hour in front of the front office cashiers before you even set foot into the office at 9 am. A nine to five hotel manager should not exist because a good deal of the days work has already slipped by before 9 am and the bulk of your customers have already gone for the day or 'gone' for good.

What are your next peaks of activity? Well, of course, a lot depends on what functions or conventions you have on for the day and when any tours are scheduled to arrive. Experience (and airline schedules) will also tell you when the bulk of your new individual arrivals will show up. On each new day you must *be prepared* to *be there*. Know your transportation arrival times – they can be very important. For example, if you are in London and running full you can expect to have an early morning problem because the bulk of North American and many other overseas flights land at Heathrow between 6.30 am and 9.00 am. Some of those tired passengers are soon to be at your front desk expecting a room. By *being there* (or by being called to come there through some pre-arranged system with the front desk) and by having made some alternative arrangements such as free use of a private lounge, washing facilities, etc. the steam can easily be taken out of the arrivals' unhappiness. It is not that the front desk clerk cannot do the job; it is just that the arrivals' self-esteem is flattered if the manager himself takes the trouble to appear on such occasions. Similarly, always plan to meet tours and conventions and make a particular point of getting close to the tour leader or convention organizer. It can save you a lot of trouble later.

Lunchtime is obviously, or hopefully, a peak but is often a good meal to sample from the customers point of view – i.e. by having lunch (*see* Chapter 13, 'Outside Looking In'). Be aware that lunch is a 'time compressed' meal (or is supposed to be for most businessmen!). At least it is more time compressed than the average dinner. Peak points at this time are such things as vehicle arrivals at your front door and the importance of parking them correctly (for the manager to be at the front door at 12.30 is often another interesting experience!) and the actual reception area of the restaurant. A few moments spent greeting regulars at the restaurant door whilst the maitre d' is struggling with his seating plan can do a lot to help the maitre d' but can also enhance the self-image of the diners whose names you have remembered. So if you are going to dine in your own restaurant make sure that you invite your guest for just after the known arrival rush has subsided – and make sure also that during your lunch you use the opportunity to 'experience' the restaurant and observe what goes on so that you can feed back the behaviour to your employees afterwards.

Early evening is also often an activity peak – particularly in bars and at the check-in desk and banquet rooms. Once again make sure that you are around to meet people as they arrive. Pick out individuals as they check in and introduce yourself to them with a warm and genuine welcome. It will surely make an impression. When were you last met by the manager of an hotel? Be certain that you have introduced yourself to the banquet organizer and if possible visit the affair and the organizer at least once during the evening. The more personal contact you make the more 'friends' you will have.

The foregoing, of course, does seem perfectly obvious but, despite that, it does so rarely seem to occur. For one reason or another hotel managers are invariably tied up with other matters at the crucial moments. It is not easy to organize oneself in the manner described above because there often seems to be more pressing things to do and to stand around in lobbies and restaurants can seem to be a waste of time. Nothing, however, that brings hotel management closer to hotel guests is a waste of time and indeed it could be saving an enormous amount of future marketing expenditure. To accomplish this type of timetable needs a great deal of self discipline, organization and discipline of other managers and supervisors. Obviously all of the other functions of management have to be fulfilled and can be. It is just that those functions which do not involve guest contact must be re-organized to fit into time slots not 'reserved' for guest contact.

Briefing and communication meetings for the day's activities can just as easily be planned to take place after the breakfast service than at its peak. Such meetings can also be disciplined not to run for very long particularly if they involve the whole supervisory group. One to one meetings between manager and department head can just as easily take place at the department head's work place as in the manager's office and, in any event, the department head is likely to feel more comfortable in his own environment. Mail and office work can surely be accomplished during mid-morning or mid-afternoon – after all once opened it is often left lying on the desk for quite a time before being attended to?

Above all, however, the discipline of *being where the action is* has some tremendous side benefits as well as that of meeting the guests. It gives the manager the opportunity, first hand, to observe the service and make the necessary adjustments. It gives him also the chance to observe his employees in action and to get to know them and for them to get to know him.

When the *being there* manager finally does get to have a meeting with his management team he will not have to hear second hand what went right or wrong the day before – he will know already; and when it comes to meetings about systems and people he will not have to be briefed on the situation – he will have seen it for himself and meetings will, therefore, take half the time and result in quicker corrective action than from a desk-bound manager.

Being there extends to the back of the house as well as to the front. The manager who from time to time asks the goods receiver to move over and does the job himself is certainly exercising superb control and the manager who empties a garbage can to look for silver plate is also just as effective.

An analysis of a purely resort hotel would, of course, produce different patterns of guest behaviour and movement from that of a city one. A prime difference from a commercial hotel is that hotel guests often have plenty of time on their hands and are not preoccupied with other things. To the business man staying in a downtown commercial hotel the quality (or lack of it) of his hotel is not likely to be the major topic in his mind at the time. To the holiday maker the quality of his hotel is very likely to be the major focus of his attention. Indeed the vacationing guest will have more time to '*be there*' and observe the action than will the hotel manager. And frequently the vacationing business man, because he may have a trained organizational mind that refuses to take a vacation, will analyse in great detail the organizational problems of the hotel whilst he is experiencing them.

In this type of hotel it is, of course, still vital that the manager *be there* but he must develop the art of not only *being there* but *being with*. In these circumstances, unlike breakfast time in a commercial hotel, the guest does seem to enjoy it if he can get to know the manager and the manager must be prepared to socialize with clients to a far greater degree. No matter what pressing problems beset the manager of a resort he must appear to have ample and unhurried time to meet and to stay with the guests. It is, of course, easy for all of them to remember who the manager is and what he looks like. It is less easy for him to remember all of them. One thing which works in his favour is that in true resort situations the guests are likely to be staying for more than a few days and, if the hotel is good, they are likely to spend a lot of time around the place, thus giving him plenty of opportunities to get to know them.

There are a few golden rules, however, and the first is simply to meet and greet everybody – or as many as is physically possible. If a call system is organized from the front desk it should not be impossible for the manager and his assistants to do just that – greet everybody; provided that the right discipline is exercised. Once that discipline is relaxed it is very hard to catch up.

The second rule is to make sure that the management say

au revoir to everybody. A few well chosen friendly words upon the departure of a guest who has been staying for the past two weeks go a long way to ensure that guests return.

In between the arrival and departure management must find a way of getting close to the guests. Formal once-a-week managers' cocktail parties are, in my view, not the best way of so doing, although these seem to be almost universally adopted in resort hotels. They are not effective because everybody comes wearing his or her 'behavioural uniform', i.e. the manager looks like the manager and probably makes a routine managers' speech of welcome. The guests all put on their best togs and turn up in the 'uniform' of guests, each one trying to outdo the next. In short there is no proper communication at these affairs.

In order to 'communicate' or get close to his guests the resort hotel manager must throw off the uniform of manager and 'join' with the guests – almost become one of them. Management can best do this by joining in with them in participative events.

For example, if any entertainment is organized (and it should be, because most people, however snobbish the environment, enjoy some form of organized entertainment, even if they only like to watch others participate), wherein guests' participation is required, then management should participate with the guests. Better still, if the management and staff of a resort hotel can participate in the entertainment of the guests, those guests will remember what a great effort management went through to give the guests a good time.

In any resort hotel for which I have been responsible I have allowed, even insisted, that senior staff eat in the same dining areas as the guests – not at the peak of business of course, but not so late that they are not seen to be there by the guests. Frequently I have found that they have been invited to sit at table with guests and I have wholeheartedly encouraged this form of guest contact. In many years I have rarely found a senior staff member abuse this privilege. It is impossible for the manager to spread himself so thin that he can get close to all the guests and that is why he needs the reinforcement of his senior staff team.

Such items as tennis tournaments, volley ball matches, bowling competitions, etc. where the staff take on the guests may sound corny but are vitally important in shaking off the 'uniform' of 'staff' which inhibits friendly communication. Staff name tags help tremendously because, in a sense, they are a way in which the hotel takes the first step, although, in this case, silently, towards communicating.

One great benefit of being so deeply involved with guests in resort hotels is that one can monitor and stay with the peaks of guest movement. When 'events' are provided in resort hotels and one participates in many of these it is easy to understand and forecast the movement and service requirements of these guests. For example, if the manager plays tennis in the tennis competition or officiates at it, he quickly comes to understand that a cool drink supply is vital during and after matches; if he is involved in showing a late night movie he quickly comes to understand that one minute after the movie finishes the lounge bar will be overcrowded and probably understaffed. In a busy resort hotel people develop patterns of behaviour. It is the manager's job to organize the staffing schedules to coincide with those patterns, not vice versa. If I could give you $100 for every time I have seen the day 'service' shift go off at 11 pm in a resort hotel when the guest movie finished at 11.15 pm you would all be rich. The management who join in with guests in events in the resort are 'working' just as hard as the manager who sits in his front lobby for half an hour looking and listening. One might be 'enjoying' himself and the other might be 'resting' but if they are doing it for the right reason and doing it in an observant fashion they will be contributing enormously to the success of their operation.

12 Don't Just Look – Look and See

'*Being there*' is not enough unless you learn to observe and *what* to observe whilst you *are* there – and unless you *stay* there long enough.

I often play a game whilst staying in hotels – a game of 'spot the manager'. It is very easy to play and managers, duty managers, assistant managers, etc. are very easy to spot. They are normally the ones in the lounge suits who walk through the hotel, avoiding any direct eye contact with the guests, keeping their own eyes in a sort of neutral position, failing to notice anything going on around them. If, as on occasion happens, they do run into a spot of trouble they normally scurry off to see to whom they can delegate the task of sorting it out. The reader may feel that this description is exaggerated, but I have witnessed this scene so many times that to me it seems commonplace. Recently I was having breakfast at an hotel in the Cayman Isles; there was a line at the door and service was very slow due to poor organization and lack of supervision. Adjacent to the breakfast room (in fact part of it, but separated by a low room divider) was a bar room. The bar was fully illuminated (brighter than the restaurant) and there, nicely spotlighted, were all of last night's dirty glasses and empty bottles. The manager – eyes in front – put in an appearance at the door of the restaurant making sure not to step past the end of the line (I suppose for fear of being recognized as the manager). In one sweeping glance he took in the scene and, having apparently failed to notice anything, slipped out of the room again and presumably carried on with his inspection tour.

Had he stepped into the restaurant he could have observed why there was a line at the door (not enough table clearers but plenty of waitresses who apparently did not include clearing tables in their duties), he would have noticed that the guests were sharing tea spoons, he would have noticed that there were no milk jugs for cereals, he would have noticed that guests were sitting at dirty tables, he would have etc., etc. – or maybe he would not have noticed anything.

There are two reasons why I noticed all these things and more. One, because I have been trained in what to look for in a restaurant. Two, because I was there long enough to spot the things that were wrong. A manager who sticks his head into a restaurant door is not *being there*. He must come into the restaurant and stay there long enough to run through a mental check list of items to see that things are in order and he must then either make a note of them for later correction or must immediately take some action which will fix them up. In an hotel there is no time like the present for fixing things. (I once had a colleague who spent so long making lists of things that were wrong in an hotel that he never had time to fix any of them!)

I also recently witnessed an even more incredible example of unobservant management in a New York establishment. Whilst waiting to be served in the restaurant I visited the men's room. It appeared that the men's facilities were used by the hotel employees as well as the guests, for prominent amongst the graffiti in the common areas of the room in very large letters it said, 'If you eat the   served in this restaurant you deserve to die – signed, the staff'. Surely the manager goes to the rest room from time to time? (And even if he does not he should, because public toilet facilities are one of the biggest tell-tale signs of the standard of management – and they are frequently neglected unnecessarily).

Like so many other things we have spoken of in this book the role of a manager requires a great deal of *self-discipline*. First, he must exercise *self-discipline* to get out where the action is and make his inspection tour. Secondly, he must exercise *self-discipline* in running through his own mental check list in each action area to see that things are just right. Thirdly he must *follow through* on things that are wrong to see that they are corrected promptly.

The *follow through* is vitally important. We have examined at great length in previous chapters the reasons for much guest contact and we have seen that given the contact the manager will certainly come away with many problems to be resolved and corrections to be made. We have also discussed how important it is that management contact with guests shall be perceived to be *sincere*. Unless action is taken by management in respect of a guest 'gripe' the manager's interest will eventually be perceived by the guest as *insincere* and all efforts made up to that point will have been useless. Problems brought to light by guests to management can only be put right, no matter how easy or complex they may be, if the manager exercises *self-discipline*. No manager can expect to be able to put everything he finds or hears wrong instantaneously and he should, therefore, write them down. Written lists of 'things to do' are in themselves a discipline. If the list gets too long you know you are in trouble; if you keep transferring items from an old list to a new one it serves to stab you with guilt. If you fail to write it down you are guaranteed to forget it if it is a task that is unpleasant or uncomfortable for you to perform and the result will inevitably be a feeling of lack of *sincerity* from the part of management to the guest.

One way, therefore, to train one's mind to cope with the mental check list required for the management inspection tour is initially to write it down – until you are so familiar with it that you will never forget it. For example the following items would appear on my restaurant check list. I am sure you can add many more.

1 *Level of lighting.* All restaurants utilized for dining at different times of the day should have lighting controls capable of being adjusted for the mood of the meal. In some cases the mood should change during the meal. Waiters sometimes have a habit of adjusting the lighting for their own purposes, not the guests.
2 *The level of noise.* If the music is coming from a live band you will invariably find they play at a volume they prefer rather than one designed for guest enjoyment. As with lights, different sound levels are appropriate for different times and different moods.
3 *The type of music.* For example, taped music should be different at 8.00 am from 10.00 pm. Waiters frequently fail

to notice that wrong tapes are playing or that tapes are slipping.

4 *The location of diners.* Headwaiters tend to spread out diners to suit the staffing stations of the restaurant. There is nothing wrong with this but restaurants should never look empty, so the correct placing of early diners is important. Similarly, restaurants, should never look closed or 'tired' so the relaying of tables when guests have gone is of vital importance, but often overlooked.

5 *The physical condition of the room.* How tidy does the room look? Are curtains neatly fixed? Are any curtains off their hooks? (They often are!) Are tablecloths all hanging at the same levels? Have the place settings been done neatly? Have extra settings been cleared away? Are waiters' sideboards in chaos? etc., etc.

6 *The state of occupied tables.* Are many tables without food or drink? Has the wine waiter visited all the tables? Are ashtrays apparent? Are condiment sets apparent? Is cutlery and crockery from the correct set (frequent problems occur in hotels of mixing sets)? Are any diners trying to catch the attention of waiters? etc., etc.

7 *The condition of staff uniforms.* Are staff wearing correct uniforms? In particular, notice shoes and socks. What condition are uniforms in, clean? Soiled?

8 *The temperature of the restaurant.* Is air conditioning functioning properly? Have men removed their jackets? etc., etc.

9 *Are controls working?* Is there an account for each table? Are duplicate checks presented with drinks? Is there a line at the cashiers? etc., etc.

I am sure you can add more and you should try to do so. Notice, however, that none of the items on my check list addresses itself to the food because although it is possible to check food quality by being in the restaurant it is probably easier to do so at the kitchen pass. Notice also how many items contribute to the success and professionalism of the restaurant other than the food itself and remember that the reason it is so important for management to check these items is because headwaiters and waiters generally perceive themselves to be in the business of serving food and are, therefore, primarily concerned with this and not with music, air conditioning, tidiness, etc. Very good waiters understand that a restaurant is a 'theatre' and the best restaurants are as much a part of showbusiness as any theatre. Good waiters, however, do get very involved with the service of their guests and because they are rushing around in the course of their duties can often be forgiven for not noticing items which are wrong with the ambiance. Take the music, for example; after working in an atmosphere of continuous music a waiter probably does not hear it any more – and with regard to the noise level once your ears have grown accustomed to one level it is easier for them to assimilate the next level up. The manager or assistant manager, however, will arrive at the scene fresh – just like the customer – and he surely ought to be able to pick up faults in the ambiance that the most experienced workers, who are permanently in that environment, will miss.

The manager on an inspection tour must develop similar mental lists for each department he visits and must discipline himself to stay long enough to check them all out. The whole process does sound exceptionally elementary and hardly worth belabouring but ask yourself from your own experiences how many restaurants you have visited with mixed holloware, dirty table cloths, draughty corners, etc., etc. The hotel business is made up of simple details but the very simplicity is deceiving because if each simple item is not attended to the results will be poor. Never believe that these tiny items are beneath you as a manager because if you ever feel that way you are assuredly in the wrong job.

At a recent conference of hotel managers which I attended, the group was asked to state honestly how often they made a complete inspection of their properties. At first most of them said 'frequently' but when the questioner became more specific and clarified his phrase 'complete inspection tour' to include a physical inspection of the entire property and everything in it from the water tanks and lift equipment on the roof, to every shower fitting in every bathroom, to every chair in every bedroom, to every piece of kitchen equipment, to every carpet in every restaurant, etc., etc. most managers had to admit that the answer was 'never'. Such an inspection, of course, could take several days. It need not be done in one stab and can be planned over a period of a few weeks but it is essential that it is done at least once per year and preferably twice.

'Why is it so important that this is done?' 'Why is it important that the manager should participate?' From a purely technical point of view such an inspection must be carried out because in most countries auditors will require that an asset register is kept and naturally they will want to know that the asset register bears some resemblance to the actual assets. Secondly, for financial planning purposes, managers will normally be required to compile estimates of future capital expenditure on an annual basis. How can this be done without an inspection of the various assets which from time to time need replacing? Why must the manager do it? In the first place because it is an excellent exercise in getting closer to the product he is selling and understanding its strengths and weaknesses. The manager is, after all, the person most directly concerned with setting standards and unless he frequently checks on the real standards being offered a huge gap can occur between the standards a manager thinks are in operation and the ones that actually exist. A manager, unless he digs a little, can often be duped by his employees into thinking that the service he gets and the rooms he is shown are typical. Employees can have a tendency to hide their errors.

Secondly, it will tell the manager much about the efficiency of his staff who are responsible for each section and will help to bring him closer to them.

Finally, when it comes to the expenditure of capital there never seems to be enough to complete the task and somebody has to decide how to use the limited amount of cash available. If the manager does not get involved in the task of deciding where the money is spent you can be sure that the spending will occur in the order of the department with the most persuasive boss down to the meekest and, for sure, the allocation of the funds will not be equitable or sensible.

The point of the foregoing is to demonstrate yet again the level of detail in which a hotel manager must get involved and the exceptional amount of *self-discipline* involved if he is to be successful. It sounds a very simple task to inspect the assets of an hotel. In fact it is a long, tedious job and one that, generally, is put off and put off until there is often not enough time to do it properly. The only way to do the job is to do it in great detail and then to follow through with the proper corrective measures. If you are not capable of coping with the 'nitty gritty' then forget hotelkeeping!

An activity as detailed as compiling an asset register should not, however, become tedious because it is not performed in a vacuum – it is performed in an hotel in the presence of staff and guests and in fact creates an opportunity for management to get to know and understand them.

Detailed observation skills are very definitely, however, the name of the game. It is so easy for the best of us to get 'lazy' in our inspection routines because 'familiarity' tends to breed a lazy eye. It does sound rather negative but if, on your inspection of the standards, you expect several things to be wrong then one useful discipline is to keep looking long enough until you find them. You surely will! In other words do not pass through an area without finding anything amiss or that can be improved. With that attitude you will keep not only your staff on their toes but yourself as well.

13 Outside Looking In

We spoke, in the last chapter, of the waiter who gets so close to his environment that he can no longer hear the music. The same can apply to a manager. You all know the saying 'He cannot see the wood for the trees'. Well, the most devoted hotel manager can, after a while, also stop 'seeing'. To guard against this occurrence hotel managers should learn the art of 'going outside to look in'.

In its most fundamental stage that is exactly what I have often suggested to managers, i.e. that they step out of their buildings and look at them from across the street. This may sound silly but it is particularly important for 'live-in' managers who rarely do just that, i.e. look at their building from the outside.

From a hotel customer's point of view, first impressions are often very important. If a good impression is created by the hotel at the outset it is easier to please the customer from then on. If a bad impression has been created the task of the 'inside' staff is naturally that much harder.

By stepping outside his own environment the hotel manager will accomplish several things.

1 He will establish how his hotel looks and sounds from the outside.
2 He will keep in touch with his competitors.
3 He will develop empathy for his guests' needs and requirements particularly inasmuch as they relate to trends and fashions.

The actual act of 'stepping outside' is almost symbolic but it leads to many things. In the first place on a purely practical level the manager looking in, provided he is observant, can share the customer's first impressions.

He can see what the doorman looks like from the outside; he can examine the state of repair of the building; he can see how the car parking works; he can see that the grounds are in order; he can see what the bedroom curtains look like from outside. I cannot begin to count the number of excellent hotels around the world that I have seen whose appearance from the outside lets them down. Have you ever observed a manager's office (which is often situated close to the entrance of the hotel), from outside, i.e. the back of filing cabinets and piles of papers pressed up against a window. Have you ever seen what store rooms look like from the outside if they have a window? Designers and architects can spend a fortune in time designing buildings that look good only to have them totally spoiled by the thoughtlessness of management and employees inside. It is a very strange thing but so many hotel managers seem to conclude that their responsibilities commence from inside the front door, not outside.

As an extension of the thought, how many managers ever try to phone their own hotels? If they did they would presumably experience the delays in answering the phone, the manner in which it is finally answered, the delays in getting them through to the right department or person and so on. How many managers phone their own hotel to make a restaurant booking? Many, when challenged, say that they do, but one wonders in that case why the problems of hotel telephone services are so commonplace.

Keeping in touch with the competition is, of course, also vital and it cannot be done properly unless the manager gets out and experiences it. In my experience many managers tend to rely on information systems for their competitive knowledge. These systems tend to be of the interhotel information sharing type where groups of local hoteliers submit such items as occupancy statistics to be shared. Other information tends to come through staff contacts at lower levels, from whence it is fed up to the manager. With regard to the sharing systems most managers tend to slightly 'pad' their figures before giving them to the competition (self-esteem?) and in the case of staff information most employees seem to tell the boss that other places are not doing very well (thereby establishing that it is not necessary to make any changes to our place since it is obviously going better than the opposition!)

One way to find out is to go out and look at other hotels. Look at the bedroom windows at night. See how many lights are on; see how many curtains are drawn; then check it out with the given statistics. Make a regular tour of the competitors' restaurants. Analyse those that are buzzing and find out why. What have they got that you are missing? Maybe a new menu, maybe a good band, maybe a great bartender? Whatever it is, find it and fix it. One thing is for sure and that is that you will never even know about it if you do not get out and see. Never be afraid to copy a good idea – especially if you can improve it!

Finally, it is important to 'get outside' to develop empathy with your guests and to educate yourself to their specific needs. It is a fact of life that many hotel managers come from an entirely different social background than their guests. An English hotel manager whose hotel caters for Argentinian tourists for example is at a disadvantage in trying to understand Argentinian needs because his background and style of life is so different from that of his guests. On a more social level it is very likely that a hotel manager will emerge from a working to middle class background whereas at the expensive end of the market his guests are likely to be from an upper middle class to upper class background. In order to be empathetic to the needs of his customer an hotel manager, at this level of the industry, must try to bridge the cultural gap.

One way, of course, if the manager can afford it (and he should be helped and encouraged to do so by his company) is to seek out and utilize the haunts of his clients so that he can fully understand and appreciate what they like. Another is to travel. Fortunately the hotel industry is truly very international and countless opportunities are offered to hotel graduates to get out and work around the world. I am continually amazed at how insular hotel school graduates tend to be. I have been fortunate in that my work (combined often with pleasure) has taken me to over seventy different countries. I may be a bit of a bore to my more insular friends and relatives and I may have missed all the benefits of a stable social life, but I have been lucky enough to develop enough common ground with many of my guests to spark off the communication process. I have also come to understand in many instances what my customers want from my hotel.

Guest questionnaire forms can be very, very helpful in the quest for good, honest feedback. Make sure, however, that they are useable and even more important make sure that the information they supply you with is used. It was always interesting to me, as the Director of a chain of hotels that utilized 'in-room' guest questionnaires, how widely the volume of completed forms varied from hotel to hotel unit. Taking common-sized units, one hotel would consistently send through 200 completed questionnaires and another 10. Some, of course, were 'conserved' by nervous staff or unit managers prior to reaching my desk but the answer was often simply that the forms were not properly displayed or 'presented' to the guests.

A golden rule in the handling of questionnaires of this sort is to respond to them. The individual guest who takes the trouble to fill in a form is opening a communication with you. Do not block it there. Respond to every single one and if possible state what action has transpired since receiving the communication. The second golden rule is to read *all* the comments and to act on them. Remember, somebody out there is telling you how they feel about you. You may disagree with them but they cannot be wrong. Not only are they the customer but they are telling you what they feel and perceive. Only they can do that and nobody can challenge them because nobody else can get into their feelings since feelings are personal things. Try to imagine a world without mirrors or reflections. How strange it would be to know what everybody else looked like but never be able to see yourself. There are plenty of 'mirrors' available to hotel managers if they look for them. Why is it, then, that they so often fail to use them? Surely they are not frightened of what they will see?

14 Mobile Control

This book cannot be complete without a word on control. Just how does hotel control fit into the behaviour pattern of the *being there* manager? How does a *being there* manager behave differently from the modern hotel trained manager of this decade and why is it that his control is superior?

Both managers rely upon accurate information systems, which mean of course that both managements must see to it that accounts and/or control departments are properly organized to produce timeous information. (This aspect of management is hardly behavioural but it is worth noting how many hotel companies with excellent guest standards have foundered on the rock of inaccurate accounts and controls.)

Both managements will only make proper use of the information if it is detailed enough and if the enquiries that it provokes from them are also detailed and demanding. In examining 'numbers' I have always found it useful to translate them continually to real items. A very famous and very rich boxer once said to me that he did not feel rich when he read his bank statement which showed he had several million dollars. He did, however, feel rich when he had five $100 bills in his back pocket. Just in the same way an item in a monthly profit and loss account such as $700 for 'guest supplies' is pretty meaningless until you break it down to the actual number of toilet rolls and tissues that it represents. You will then find yourself asking how is it that in your hotel every guest 'backside' uses two toilet rolls per day! It is only when the figures are read properly in this way that they start to be useful and highlight areas of potential problems.

I once did some consulting work for the owners of a new luxury hotel in Chicago. It was the owners' first venture into the hotel world and they came from a business where percentages seemed to mean more than actual items. They had a beautiful property but were doing very badly on the bottom line. Their sales (rooms and food and beverage) prices were very high and therefore some of the percentage costs did not seem out of line, but after a cursory glance at the real items one saw that, for example, there must have been an enormous amount of pilfering of holloware. The actual cash figure involved did not seem to frighten or worry the owners until my colleague thought of the idea of piling the equivalent number of silver teapots that had disappeared daily on to the boardroom table. The table was not big enough! – and the owners certainly got the message.

On another occasion I was visiting the commercial director of an airline who had not focused on the smaller type of expenses of his business, presumably because airlines talk big, big numbers in purchasing the actual planes and because their major expenditures are on people and fuel. By dividing such miscellaneous items as toothpicks, cloth head rests, tissues, glasses, etc. into the number of flying passengers we came up with some astonishing figures indicating gross waste or misuse or downright robbery. In his airline it seemed it was commonplace for each passenger to use five toothpicks, three headrests, break two glasses and so on. To me it was astounding that those calculations had never been focused on before. This style of control or this attitude is called 'back to zero'. A common error in control and budgetary procedure is to assume that historical usages are correct and to use them as a measurement for current performance. From time to time it is useful to throw away the historical data and to get back to basics because after a while an original error is compounded until there is so much 'fat' one could float on it.

This is not a book on hotel accounting (there are plenty available), and I will not therefore dwell on the subject but I must repeat that the production of correct and up-to-date accounts is absolutely vital to the success of any hotel venture – or in fact any other business venture of any sort.

As an hotel manager you have not been hired as an accountant and shall not become one but you have a primary duty to ensure that somebody is effectively handling the accounts function.

As an hotel manager do not let accounting deadlines slip past. Late or 'catch up' accounting is invariably inaccurate because memories fade and personnel change. Be vigorous in your demand for timely information.

As an hotel manager do not tolerate useless information. The actual writing up of the books should not be of great concern to you (provided they balance properly) except in as much that their format leads to a useful financial reporting format to you that you can readily understand and yet is in sufficient detail for you to exercise detailed control.

The format should allow for comparisons with previous time periods and budgeted performance. It should not contain vague and general categories such as 'miscellaneous' or 'sundry'. (Those words were banned from any financial review I used to conduct!) It should, however, only contain information that you can use. Challenge every figure as to its usefulness and beware of pen pushers who provide you with reams of analysis from whence you can take no action.

In reviewing your current accounts ask the question 'why?' at least one hundred times and ask it again when you get the answer. Just as in checking and observing 'standards' assume that you will find several areas where savings could have been made and keep looking until you find them. You surely will!

It is at this point that the *being there* manager and the 'modern' manager probably part company. The 'modern' manager will almost certainly be causing more information to be produced than he can cope with and the more he tries to cope the more involved he becomes with the quest of perfecting the information for the sake of a perfect system rather than concentrating on what the information is for. And, the more time he spends in analysis of the information the less time he spends with his guests and staff and the more out of touch he becomes. At the same time his information becomes more and more out of date and eventually, given the natural progression of this chain of events, he starts trying to lock the stable door after the horse has bolted.

Control can be expensive. There is no point in spending more money on control procedures than you can actually save by the controls. (As one of seventeen control clerks at the Grosvenor House hotel in 1961 I never quite 'saved' the company an amount per week that was equal to my weekly salary – nor did the other sixteen!)

The *being there* manager will concentrate on keeping the horse in the stable by slamming the door in his face or by discovering that the door is unlocked before the horse does. As we have seen the *being there* manager will discipline himself to be where the action is – and, in this case, the action relative to waste and control. He will work well with a few well-tried principles i.e. he will want to co-sign all cheques (so he knows what is being spent at the time of spending), he will frequently change locks and keys to all storerooms, he will physically get involved from time to time in the wage pay out at the 'window', he will physically from time to time get involved at the receiving bay, he will be irregular with his visits (sometimes he will show up in the middle of the night or very early in the morning), and he will see to it that stocks are kept as low as possible. If the par stock of turkeys in the deep freeze is 6 it is easy to see if 2 are missing; if the chef or buyer have got a 'good deal' on 600 turkeys you will never see easily if 60 go astray and all of a sudden a 'good deal' is not so good after all. (Besides which it may be better to have the cash than the turkeys!)

Once again this type of physical control which catches things as they happen rather than analysing them afterwards demands that the manager is *observant*. The manager watching a barman at work must be able to observe the way he pours, the way he rings up, etc. The manager padding down a bedroom floor corridor must 'take in' the remains on the breakfast trays. Why was the wrong thickness serviette used here, the wrong size juice glass here, a four person size milk jug for a single room, etc., etc?

Physical surveillance plays a major aspect in all areas of hotel control. Without such surveillance the task of the controller is meaningless. Hotel companies have frequently searched for controllers who are not only book-keepers but who are also prepared to get into the hotel and physically observe what goes on. The search is often in vain – because by the same token that it is exceptionally difficult to find an hotel manager who can move from one to ten on our admin/mobile scale, it is even more difficult to find a book-keeper who is willing to forgo the books temporarily for a good look around the action.

For this reason it is all the more important for hotel managers to be mobile. During their movements they and their assistants will normally have to exercise that physical control surveillance that the controllers are unable or often unwilling to do.

For example, a controller might frequently report that an entertainment bar with a cover charge averages 100 'entrances' per night. A mobile manager if he is observant can in a flash count the number of bodies in the bar at any moment as a physical check. Without that check there is no control – only pieces of paper. In fact physical surveillance is an essential part of all revenue controls.

The very real problem of hotel control is that all the materials used by hoteliers are so useful and readily usable by all of the employees. They are also very transportable – be they linen, cutlery, food, whatever. The process of real control however is relatively simple because 'loss' can only occur if the goods were paid for but did not arrive, were consumed by people who did not pay for them (including staff), or were removed from the premises by staff or guests unlawfully.

The mobile manager can control staff because that small percentage who want to steal will know that danger of surveillance always lurks around the corner. If the manager is glued to his office chair the potential pilferers will have plenty of room and time for manoeuvre. A mobile manager will visit the staff canteen to see what is being eaten (in fact a mobile manager will frequently eat in the staff canteen for more reasons than simply 'control') and a mobile manager will see that employees are being searched (where law allows) at the back door – (and he will insist that *all* staff utilize the same exit and are subject to equal treatment).

The mobile manager will start seeing waste as it occurs. The mobile manager will start knowing the habits of his employees; he will see who flashes money around or hear of who takes luxury cruises or indulges in tastes beyond the reasonable reach of the salary. (I once became suspicious of a hall porter because I saw him park his Ferrari a few streets from the hotel! He was caught soon after entering a room with a false master key and police inspection of his apartment later revealed many stolen items.) In short, the same traits which help the manager keep observation on guest standards will help him control the business.

The mobile manager should not need to ask his assistants or controller why the figures say what they do one month after the event – he should know already!

15 Can the Personnel Function Survive?

The reader may be forgiven at this point for wondering what is the future of such service departments as personnel and marketing, if the 'superman' mobile manager is being all things to all people. Have I not stated in earlier chapters that training is the responsibility of line management and have I not stated that the need for marketing will diminish in many instances if the hotel manager attends to maintaining standards? In that case, do we need service departments and if so, what will be their role?

A personnel function in an hotel is required beyond any doubt. Whether that function takes up the full-time employment of one or more people, thus rendering it a service department, or whether it is the part-time responsibility of a particular member of management depends upon the size of the hotel. Irrespective of hotel size, however, and notwithstanding the style of the hotel manager, the need for the function always exists.

If the hotel is fortunate enough to be under the charge of a particularly mobile manager, certain aspects of the personnel function will be reduced – particularly the requirement for the personnel manager to have to translate to the hotel manager the 'feelings' of the personnel. On the other hand, an hotel manager, who is aware of the feelings of his employees and their standards of performance from first-hand observation, is likely to be the sort of manager who will place high emphasis on team building and standards training, thereby applying a heavy work load on to his personnel manager.

Not all managers are, of course, as mobile as this book advocates and in many instances they just do not get to their employees or are incapable of 'hearing' them. When this happens the 'translating' role of the personnel manager is vital. The very fact that the personnel manager is a third party creates a channel through which employee feelings can flow (this is why part-time line – part-time personnel managers often fail in this aspect). Employees will say much to a personnel manager (third party) that they will not say to their boss (however mobile he is) especially until they have established an open relationship with the boss.

A mobile manager will, of course, find more time for employee contact than other managers – and in so doing will break down the barriers of communication with his employees, so that they will become open and frank. However, with the best will in the world and however good a listener the manager may be, the fact is that there will simply not be time to 'hear' everybody. Two other circles need to be concentrated upon, not just that of human resources. Meanwhile the personnel manager can concentrate primarily on the human resource aspect of the business and he is one man in the organization who is not called upon to answer the call of the guest – except of course in a secondary manner.

The personnel manager is also interdepartmental – just like the hotel manager. From this privileged position he can observe the performance and interaction of the hotel 'cells' and he is therefore in a perfect position to diagnose problems and weaknesses in the team and to plan remedial team building. The very impartiality of the personnel manager's position is what makes it so vital in effecting team building exercises. For example, the extensive team building exercises carried out in the late sixties at the Carlton Tower would not have taken place without the input of a personnel department who was able to diagnose a problem, design a cure and assist in administering it.

This third party aspect of personnel management is also of great importance in another respect. It is the ongoing duty of the personnel manager, irrespective of the style of the manager, to be the conscience of the organization. When the profit motive is concerned, managers can frequently jeopardize long-term advantages for short-term profits. This happens, of course, not only with regard to employees but also with regard to standards. How often has one seen short-term savings – particularly with regard to repairs and maintenance and capital replacements – being made at the expense of the long-term reputation of the company? The same is true of short-term savings concerning employees. Unfair or excessively harsh treatment of staff today to save a 'bob or two' can result in long-term disadvantage. Apart from which unfair treatment of staff should be avoided on purely moral and ethical grounds. The personnel manager is the one person in the organization who *must* shout UNFAIR! if line management has indulged, either knowingly or not, in such treatment. This policing role is very important.

A second policing role is far more commonly required, i.e. disciplining everybody else in the organization re personnel affairs. Earlier in this book we refer to the task setting procedure known as MBO. Without an interdepartmental person organizing such a system it will fail. The personnel manager will find it necessary to nag everybody concerned, including the hotel manager, in order to make the system work. Without disciplinary action, reminders, help and encouragement from a personnel director, MBO systems invariably fall down. With proper organization and discipline they can contribute tremendously to the success of a venture.

The same is true with regard to employee appraisal systems. A mobile manager will appear to have less need for formal appraisals because he is close to his employees and giving them constant feedback. This is not so, for a regular formal appraisal of an employee's performance, away from the pressures of the job, can only be beneficial to improving the employee's performance and the relationship between the manager and the employee. The fact that there has been ongoing contact and feedback will enhance the quality of the appraisal session because the manager will have many examples of employee behaviour to draw upon and the employee will only be able to relate to specific examples. An 'administrative' type of manager will not be able to conduct an appraisal too easily because he will only have second-hand examples and the employee will reject criticism with 'what does he know about it? He's never around when the pressure's on!'

In the instance of appraisals you can be sure they will never take place unless the personnel function disciplines line management to carry them out. They do not just happen; they need organizing and scheduling and in some cases the two participants need a third (neutral) party present to help them along.

Discipline and organization from the personnel department are also required with regard to training. It is true that this book stresses the responsibilities of line management with regard to training, but it also recognizes that, whereas line managers can be taught how to train, they are not necessarily specialists in the design of training programmes – nor even if they had the ability could they possibly have the time to create the necessary designs. We have also seen that people seem to learn from competent line managers better than from training specialists – but somebody has to prepare the material for we have also seen that training materials must be in such detail and so specific that trainees can relate to them. The detailed design and construction of training programmes is clearly the job of the personnel and training specialist because it requires time, diligence and imagination that would be difficult for the most mobile of managers to spare. In fact the very mobility of a manager rules him out from the painstaking task of preparing training material.

Discipline is also required with regard to the actual training. Line management often seems to display resistance to releasing personnel for training sessions. Training cannot be haphazard. It requires detailed organization and then requires someone to exercise the necessary discipline to make sure that it is attended and followed up. That is the role of a personnel manager.

The hotel personnel manager must also be a tidy administrator because poor records can result in very unhappy employees and good records can be a terrific boon. I once worked for an hotel manager who made a diary note of all of his employees' birthdays and sent them all a birthday card. It may sound a bit corny but actually you could not really object to receiving a birthday card – just as you cannot really object to receiving a compliment – because it makes you feel good. Where did he get his birthday dates from? From the personnel records, of course, and only because the personnel manager had made sure the employee files were all correctly filled in.

More crucial than birthdays are of course payroll and timekeeping records. No matter how good a mobile manager is at knowing his employees, he cannot possibly keep in his head all the information and promises that relate to or have been made to all the employees. Accurate records are essential and many excellent manager/employee relationships have temporarily broken down because employees have received the wrong increase or the wrong wage packet or the wrong deductions. It is clear, therefore, that in the area of administration the personnel function, be it delegated to an assistant manager with other responsibilities in a small unit, or be it full time, is still required however mobile the hotel manager is.

Finally, there is the question of recruitment, from within and without. People are a very, very important asset to an hotel company, although not necessarily *the* most important, because they do tend to come and go and can be replaced and retrained (although at great expense). Protecting that asset is therefore as important as protecting the bricks and mortar and furniture. The personnel manager should be in charge of the 'protection'. He should carry in his head – and on paper (in case he too gets moved on), an inventory of the human asset. He should know the hopes and aspirations, strengths and weaknesses of all those within his realm and when opportunities or vacancies occur he should be in a position to make the necessary recommendations for promotion from within the ranks. He should also keep an eye on the outside world because invariably he will be forced to look outside for new recruits.

It is obvious that the person he wishes to recruit is more than likely working for somebody else, i.e. if he is currently out of work (except in unusual circumstances) he is probably not the right person. It is also logical that the pick of the employees that he would like to recruit are working for his most successful opposition. The mobile manager will, as we have seen in the chapter on 'outside looking in' be visiting the competition frequently. One of the things he can be looking for is who are the best employees. Far better to see your potential future employees on the job than evaluate their skills in an interview. There is no reason therefore that the personnel function should not also be making forays into competitors' territory. They will find it a far more cost-effective method of recruiting than the small (or sometimes large and expensive) ads.

The screening interview, however, can never be completely replaced and the personnel manager should realize that an enormous burden is placed upon his shoulders because although line management should, and often do, actually make the choices they always rely very heavily upon the 'professional' views of the professional interviewer – the personnel manager. It is exceptionally easy to take on the wrong person to fill an urgent gap. It is not so easy to make amends for the wrong doings of the wrong person and it is sometimes not too easy to get rid of them.

16 The Role of Marketing

In an earlier chapter the role of an hotel marketing function was virtually dismissed on the basis that a well-run hotel, particularly if it were to be in the repeat business market, would eventually need almost no sales, public relations or advertising support at all. This is, perhaps, an exaggeration, for any hotel, however well run, would have to be located in a perfect spot in perfectly favourable economic conditions to be able to operate at ultimate efficiency without marketing activity back-up.

The fact is, of course, that economic and social conditions are changing continuously and the perfectly-run product may meet the market requirements one year but miss by a mile, the next. There can, however, be no question that a hotel renowned for its excellent standards will have minimal marketing expenditure whatever the prevailing economic conditions are whereas a hotel that is unable to build repeat business due to poor standards will continually have to search for new and possibly more expensive-to-get-to markets. This is true for both city and resort hotels.

No matter how well managed and no matter how high the standards are, certain hotels will still need marketing. New hotels, for example, need time for their reputation to spread and until that happens they will need to be marketed strongly. Seasonal hotels need to be filled off-season and international hotels have frequently to replace markets according to the ebb and flow of national economies.

The role of the hotel marketing function is, regrettably, far too complex to be covered in one chapter of this book – it is a complete

The Role of Marketing 117

book in itself. Hotels come in too broad a range of shapes, sizes, types, location, markets, countries and environments to be able to write easily and succinctly about how they should be marketed. I, therefore, propose to examine briefly the marketing role only in the light of other things which have been written herein.

Refer again to the figure of hotel management activity on p. 320

You will recall that marketing activity, as it is described in this volume, is truly a service or support role – independent of the ongoing activities of our mobile manager. It therefore has far less immediate relationships with the style of management being preached herein because it is not an integral part of the mainstream activity – which, as we have just seen, is not the case with regard to the personnel support function.

Behavioural science, however, does have much to teach the hotel marketing executive. In fact the whole cornerstone of his thinking should revolve around peoples' needs, desires and behaviours. The marketing man generally has the following tools at his disposal – advertising, public relations activity, and a sales force. He must find ways of using each of these tools so that they will be successful with due regard to the nature of the customer he is trying to attract.

The most important thing for a hotel marketing executive to determine is the position of his product in the market.

For example, he should clearly understand which of Maslow's human needs on the hierarchy (or guest needs as they are described here) he is trying to reach with his policies and advertisements. He should understand fully just where his product is positioned on this hierarchy. The most successful worldwide advertising campaign for Holiday Inns simply stated that 'There are no surprises at a Holiday Inn'. In other words the 'Holiday' marketing people were clearly recognizing that the Holiday Inn product was aiming to satisfy the low level security needs – i.e. no surprises – unpleasant and perhaps even pleasant. Westin Hotels on the other hand extensively advertise that 'No two Westin Hotels are the same'. Here the advertisers are obviously aiming at satisfying 'self-esteem'. In the early days of Southern Sun, Sol Kerzner, the Managing Director, dreamt up a magnificient phrase that hit straight at the second level of Maslow's hierarchy; it simply said 'Southern Sun Hotels – you can feel the warmth'.

These are examples of how the marketing man can 'position'

his hotel by the messages he sends out to the public through advertising.

It is more subtle, but he can also position an hotel or chain of hotels through clever public relations work, particularly if it is decided that the product is to be up-market. We have seen earlier that people get 'satisfaction' from staying at the right address, but how are they – or more important, how are the people they think are watching them – to *know* that they are at the right address. One way of course is to let it be known that famous and desirable people also stay at the address. A casual mention on the radio, a picture of a celebrity recognizably at the establishment, an in-house, in-room journal showing all the famous people who have 'slept here before you' – all of these are powerful ways to enhance self-esteem.

I can recall vividly the opening of the Landdrost Hotel in Johannesburg in 1973. Here was a case of knowingly positioning an hotel through public relations work. My company was forced to take over the lease of the Landdrost (before it was called that) as part of the takeover of another hotel company. The hotel, which is not very well located in the town, was being built as a two to three star hotel with coffee shop, function room, and about 300 bedrooms. It was quickly realized that due to the rent of the building it could never be made to pay as a three star operation even if it were 100 per cent occupied. Last minute action was taken to convert about fifty rooms to suites, add three speciality restaurants, inclusive of a dance and cabaret room and to upgrade the property generally.

The major competition was Western International's (latterly Westin's) Carlton Hotel – a 600 room modern American style hotel in the best location in town. The Carlton enjoyed five star rating and was well established as the leading hostelry in town.

The location of the Landdrost was infinitely inferior and although its new decor and spaces had been deliberately designed to contrast with the brashness of the Carlton, it was decided that a major public relations job had to be undertaken to convince the public that all the best people stayed at the Landdrost, not the Carlton, and that therefore the Landdrost was *really* the best address in town. Even before the day of opening a deliberate attempt was made to track down every celebrity – be they sportsmen, film stars, politicians or whatever and to get them to stay at the hotel – to pamper them when they were there so that they would want to return and then to let everybody know through the appropriate media channels where they were.

For about three years the Landdrost successfully cornered the market on visiting celebrities to Johannesburg and it was not long before it was considered to be the fanciest address, with the result that room rates were continually raised making also the highly profitable venture that it could never have been as a 'middle of the road' property.

I have touched upon advertising and public relations but what about the third tool – the sales personnel? Most hotel groups and many individual large hotel units employ sales personnel whose job it is to go forth into the wide world beyond the lobby of the hotel or the corporate offices of the hotel company to solicit business.

Several factors of relevance to this book are worth noting in connection with hotels sales persons. First, nowhere in the universe of hotelkeeping can the interdepartmental chasm be so wide as it often is between sales and operations people. There often seems to be a natural barrier between operations and sales personnel. It is, of course, not difficult to see why – for are not the sales personnel the unruffled well-dressed ones, always wining and dining on the company's money and on the fruits of the labour of the rest of us; are not sales personnel the ones who always promise the impossible but are rarely around to make sure that the impossible is achieved; are not sales personnel the very ones who after the event is all over arrive with all the trifling little complaints?

This particular interface is a very difficult one indeed and it is therefore essential for the hotel manager to recognize their potential danger and think 'team building' from the outset. It is essential for operations personnel to understand the nature of the job of a sales person and it is likewise essential for a sales person to understand the difficulties and limitations of the production and service staff. The first job of a hotel sales person is not therefore to 'sell' himself to the operations personnel but to 'reveal' himself. He or she must demonstrate that they are individuals, chasing the same goal as the operators, but wearing a different 'uniform' and with obviously different sets of skills. Only real time spent with each other and real efforts to understand each others' difficulties and aspirations can overcome the potential gap between the two, especially since the daily work routine of each, constantly throws out potential traps to their teamwork. Lesson number one, therefore, to a budding hotel salesman is to spend at least as much time with your non-sales colleagues as you do with your clients. If the potential sore between salesman and operator is allowed to fester the inevitable loser is, of course, the hotel guest.

Other factors to be noted are the nature of the product being sold and the nature of the buyer. Unlike most sales jobs the product here for sales is rather intangible. Often promises, not physical objects, are being sold. The very notion of having hotel specialized salesmen is foreign and rather new to many people, yet the thought of, say, car salesmen is not hard to grasp. A car salesman is actually selling something tangible (although often complete with many promises!) whereas the hotel salesman is selling a future service. This fact can lead to excessive anxiety on the behalf of the buyer.

Such anxiety also exists in the buyer of a tangible object, but this anxiety is quickly dispelled once he finds the car or the fridge, etc. actually work. The anxiety of the hotel services buyer will linger on until the day the sale is consumated or in the case of 'multi-sales' until good experiences cause him to relax.

Note also that the buyer is often buying on behalf of others, i.e. a personnel director to run a seminar, a mother and father for their daughter's wedding, a secretary for a visiting VIP, etc. – and they have all heard many, many stories about what goes wrong in hotels. They are buying for and worried about a host of different things on Maslow's scale ... will the hotel do it right so that I make the best impression?, will they keep his room after midnight?, and so on.

How can the sales person eliminate the fears of the buyer? First, by making sure that he has got the details of the purchase correct, secondly by making sure that the details have been correctly and painstakingly passed and understood by the operations personnel, and thirdly by reassuring the client that all this has been done. In the end, hotelkeeping often comes back to the same thing – attention to detail – and the role of a sales person is no different from anybody elses' in the hotel in this respect. A final detail, if it is physically possible and depending upon the type of sale made, is for the salesperson to put in an appearance at the event and thereafter to follow up with an after sales call. Both activities show a 'caring' that will be appreciated.

A final thought on the subject, but one that has worked well for me in the past. Take a hotel salesman and build him from time to time into the roster of hotel duty management. Likewise, take an hotel manager or assistant and from time to time send him out with a salesman on the road. The mutual respect they develop for each other will be very healthy.

17 Designing for People

For a long while the subject of hotel design has intrigued me. When I was at 'hotel school' this subject was touched upon from time to time but always from the point of view of the efficiency of the work force. For example, bedroom designs became dominated by the requirements of the staff to keep them clean. I can remember being 'shown over' the then new Post House concept in England with its rather utilitarian unit furniture; the dressing tables, desks and drawer units never seemed to have legs and were cantilevered from the wall so that the maids could clean under them easily.

Discussions of kitchen, restaurant and front desk design at my college were dominated by the functional requirements of the area. In other words the whole emphasis on my design teaching was from a functional point of view rather than from an analysis of the needs of the guest.

It slowly became apparent to me as the years of practical experience passed that the 'impact' of a design was vitally important, that correct ambiance was absolutely necessary and that colours, shapes, materials, etc. were more important from the point of view of pleasing the guest than from the point of view of saving a maid's aching back. Many architects and interior designers over the last couple of decades have exploited fully and well the self-esteem needs of the clients and some splendid work has been achieved.

The greatest learning and achievement has been the designers' recognition of the fact that people like to be with people. As a resident of New York I am certain that the main attraction of this great city is its people – not its buildings. To observe the sidewalks of New York is to witness an ongoing parade, sometimes amusing, sometimes sad, but always full of interesting sights. These people are crammed into the tiny island of Manhattan – the focal point of an otherwise sprawling city.

As a frequent visitor to Paris I cannot help but be fascinated by the Champs Elysee and all the other areas of pavement cafes and restaurants. As a visitor to Milan one cannot help but feel the excitement of the Galleria! And so on around the world.

I was once involved in New York in a very lengthy and tiring business negotiation in order to promote a boxing match between Muhammed Ali and Leon Spinks. The participants in the negotiation included a tall 'show-biz type' New York black man, a rather sheltered lawyer from New York, another from South Africa, and myself. Late one evening we decided to break off our negotiations and go to eat. Gregory, the black, volunteered to make a table reservation at a popular upper East side restaurant. When we got there it was packed with a line outside and people obviously waiting at the bar. We were ushered straight to a table smack bang in the middle of the room. 'My goodness', exclaimed the South African lawyer to Gregory, 'You can see everything from here!' 'No', retorted Gregory, 'Everyone can see *you* from here!' It is this that the designers of hotels seem to have learned – and the principal benefit therefore has been in the public areas of the hotels they have designed.

Even kitchen design has, in some instances, been modified to appeal to customers rather than to remain purely functional. In cheap restaurants there has been a great movement towards 'open' kitchens where the customer can see what is going on. Many resort hotels have developed successfully the concept of semi-buffet style meals where the chefs in fact finish cooking procedures in front of the guests and 'meet' the guests as they serve them. This renewal of contact between chef and diner is indeed a vindication of the importance of staff/guest communication as discussed earlier.

In one highly priced New York restaurant, there is a glass wall between the kitchen and the restaurant. One large dining table is situated in a little alcove adjacent to the window; it is a very popular table.

The concept of a focal point in hotel design is, however,

exceptionally important but it is a concept that for a period during the last few decades was missed. During the era of the development of the international high rise chains (mainly by airline company subsidiaries) the design from this point of view was often terrible. Hotel residents were split up and herded into separate compartments of restaurants and lounges. The lobbies were often cold and uninteresting. The guests were segmented into a coffee shop on the ground floor, a restaurant on the next floor, a bar on the top floor, etc., i.e. no focal point – no meeting point. (Bars and night clubs on top floors were built all over Europe and all were and still are, in some cases, disasters. People like to go 'down' to night clubs and to look in. In any event you cannot see out of windows at night!) The strange thing was that examples of hotel focal points from many old hotels were staring the designers in the face (e.g. the Palm Court at the Plaza, New York) but errors continued to be made and still are in many new properties.

The single most innovative chain of hotels over the last two decades from a point of view of design based on behavioural study is undoubtedly Club Mediterranee: 'Club Med'-built villages with social centres. The social centre always included a restaurant, bar, dance floors, bandstand, pool and games room, and open-air theatre. In nearly all cases it is possible to see into each of these entities from another. At a 'Club Med' you can be in the action or watch the action but you need never be out of it unless you choose to be and for those 'quiet times' you can sit on a lonely beach on your own in the tranquillity or listen to classical music at sunset.

The largest of these hotels and indeed the style of service took into consideration the needs of people on vacation. Telephones in rooms were dispensed with, there were no formal dress requirements, regular money was not utilized (you could buy beads with money when you arrived and these would be exchanged at the bar or for other hotel purchases and food and wine). All sporting activities were included in the price so once one had paid in advance and arrived there could be no more money worries. Meals are only served at tables of eight and diners are obliged to fill up vacant table spaces until tables of eight are full. Unless you happen to be with a party of seven friends you are therefore forced to sit with (and therefore meet) other people on vacation. The whole concept was, when it was first conceived, extremely daring but it worked. 'Club Med' now has over ninety resorts throughout the world and has satisfied a need of a whole section of the vacation market that was not being met before.

But what should be the hotel design of the future? Already in the US there is a movement from the massive chain hotels of the sixties and seventies to smaller more personal hotels. John Colman, a wealthy medicine packager, is proving the point, with his move into the hotel industry by his purchase and renovation of several old, but small, hotel buildings. Colman is touting a return to personal service and the returns from his Fairfax hotel in Washington would seem to indicate that this is what the public want and probably always did. Hyatt has also started to develop a chain of smaller more intimate hotels.

Consideration for hotel design of the future, of course, transcends the potential psychological needs of the guest. Amongst other things to be considered for future city hotels are these.

The future changes in transportation patterns
Will the ever decreasing supply of oil limit air travel as we know it or will other fuels be developed? Concorde already speeds up travel and can eliminate hotel nights? Although unsuccessful at this stage what will the next SST be able to do? What will replace the motor car? What will all this do to the shape of our cities?

The changing face of cities
During the last two decades the downtown areas of many cities became unsafe and unsavoury. Citizens tended to move to the suburbs and with them went shopping centres, cinemas and hotels. For example, in 1978 the occupancy of St Louis' suburban hotels was at least 15 per cent higher than those downtown – a pattern often repeated throughout North America. During the late 1970s this trend began to be reversed and certain US cities have experienced a boom in downtown real estate. Will this trend continue? Will the same problems beset other international cities? Just what will the future bring? These questions are very real and crucial to hotel developers. One only has to look at the fate of the grand railway hotels spread across Europe to realize how changes in cities and transportation patterns affect the hotel industry.

Development in communication
What will improved communication do to the hotel industry? Conversations on the telephone are still not a good enough substitute for face-to-face communication (although conference call systems do eliminate certain business travel) because the voice is only part of the communication process. But what will happen when another part of the process is added to the phone? TV phones are already a certainty. What effect will they have on business travel?

The increase in women executives
More and more women are working. Will more and more women become executives and travel as a part of their work? What do women want from a hotel room than men do not?

The trends in mix of guests
The US hotels have had an exceptionally heavy volume of convention room nights. Tourism has continued to be a growth industry throughout the world. Will these trends continue? Will they spread to other countries? Have we reached a peak of world travel due to increased costs? For what mix of guests will we be building the hotels of the future?

The answers to these items will determine what future guests want from a hotel room but there are also factors which determine what services and facilities hotels will be able to provide. As we have discussed earlier in this book in the chapter on job satisfaction, hotel employment is deemed by many to be servile and therefore the difficulty in attracting hotel workers becomes more severe in developed countries.

Correspondingly, the difficulty and costs of providing service in a labour-intensive way will increase. The rise in building costs in excess of the inflation rate will also go a long way to dictating what can be provided. We could be saying *au revoir* to the era of architectural fantasy and hello to the era of practical renovation.

I am in no better position than anyone else to predict accurately the most propitious route future hotel developers should take, but an analysis of what we now provide and a cross check to see if it, right now, is meeting the needs of our guests might be a good place to start, for if we are behind the times now, a new developer who does not repeat the old mistakes will at least be ahead of the game.

What are the needs of a transient individual at a city hotel? He or she could have a combination of the following requirements from an hotel room:

office space and facilities
sleeping accommodation
information
entertainment
meeting other people
gymnasium or keep-fit facility
travel arrangement services
sex
religious help

etc., etc.

What are the types of transient people who might frequent our hotel?

business executives on short stays, 1-3 nights
business executives on medium stays, 4-14 nights
business executives on long stays, over 2 weeks
relocating families
male transient
female transient
short-stay tourist
longer-stay tourist
group or convention
chief executive level
other executive level
different nationalities

etc., etc.

Are existing city hotels meeting all of these requirements for all these types of people? Answer – no!

The existing hotels in the main are buildings with bedrooms and public areas. As mentioned earlier the design of public areas has in many cases gone a long way to meet quite a few of guests' needs but in others the spending on public areas and architecture has gone overboard whereas the development of the other facilities, particularly room design, has been neglected. Most hotels have 'boxes' for rooms with bathrooms included. The predominant feature in most hotel rooms is the bed or, more likely, the beds. Hallways are invariably long and thin with bedrooms off either side and suites often at the ends. Hotel rooms are almost always of identical size to all the other rooms in the hotel having been built as 'units'. Suites are often two or three units joined together.

This system tends to limit each hotel to satisfying the needs of one type of guest rather than another, to one 'length of stay guest' rather than another, and so on. This naturally limits the market of that particular hotel and increases the number of guests, who despite staying at the hotel, are not completely satisfied.

An interesting point is that although people do travel in groups of like need, the market segment of each type of group may be quite small or at least too small to deserve an hotel to meet its specific requirement. Also, within groups travelling together, there are often many different requirements.

Imagine yourself as a young executive of a large corporation travelling on business with the Chairman of the Board. He may need to stay for the image of the company at the Inn on the Park and his budget will allow for it. Your budget only allows you to stay at the Penta – but you need to be in the same hotel as him for reasons of communication. Neither hotel can meet your joint needs.

Picture the average tourist group on a 'package' tour. A honeymoon couple, two secretaries sharing, a young executive and his wife, an old lady with a stick, etc. How can the needs of this group possibly be identical? How can one hotel satisfy such a variety of needs?

Hotels, as we all know, are exceptionally capital hungry – so are aeroplanes. Cannot the aeroplane industry teach the hotel developer something? Aeroplane travellers are the same people who will eventually stay in your hotel – or a market segment of them. By and large they cannot choose different aeroplanes to satisfy their needs so the aeroplane has to be adapted, hence the proliferation in recent years of various classes of travel. Most transatlantic carriers now have a luxury first class section, a full paying business class section, and an economy tourist section on the same plane.

I predict that the first city hotels to go in this direction will be successful, i.e. the first hotels which try, through physical planning, to adapt to the behavioural requirement of a range of guests will be winners.

Why do hotel rooms in the same hotel all have to be identical? To make purchasing easier? To assist with staff scheduling? Nonsense. They do not have to be! Future hotel complexes could include:

rooms designed and equipped for overnight stays
rooms designed and equipped for day and overnight stays
lounge or office type suites for longer stays
apartments for period rental
'first class' accommodation wings with superior service
'economy class' accommodation wings
office block for short, medium and long leases
gymnasiums
health clubs
sports facilities
clinics
adult education centres
convention and meeting rooms
cinemas
live entertainment areas
shops – open at useful hours
transport booking facilities
car hire centres
hairdressing and beauty salons
chapels
banks – at useful hours
tourist information centres
variety of food and drink outlets

Hotel rooms could be designed according to categories within the same building.

Short-stay rooms

1 The bed must not be the predominant feature
2 Low requirement for two beds
3 A lounge or office concept
4 Flexibility of lighting, e.g. office and evening levels
5 Limited storage
6 Luggage racks designed to fit modern luggage
7 Security features
8 In-room lock-up facilities
9 'Fantasy' type rooms

10   Convenient telephone designs – flexicord, push button, TV connected, etc.
11   TV, dial a video, new services, telephone linked
12   In-room feeding and drinking mechanisms
13   Women's requirements
14   Clothes pressers
15   Hi fi systems, tape selections
16   'Brighter' decor
17   Improved bed designs
18   Improved linen design, i.e. duvets, no press, etc.

Longer-stay rooms
Consider the following in addition to or in place of items in short-stay rooms:
1   Larger room or extra room (i.e. all suite)
2   Eating area
3   Working area
4   Additional lounging space
5   Additional storage space
6   More subdued decor for longer stay
7   Self-catering facilities – ice, mechanized bar
8   Less staff disturbance, maid service on demand, not according to maid's schedule
9   Daily linen changes really necessary?
10   Different soap size?
11   Different towel size?
12   Separate W.C.'s?
13   'Dressing' areas
14   Proper itemized telephone accounts
15   Ironing boards?

First class rooms
Consider the following:
1   Separate area of hotel
2   Separate check in
3   Separate luxury lounges
4   Larger rooms or suites only
5   Club feeling

etc., etc.
  The multi-purpose hotel will, of course, never replace the

small exclusive unit which is still able to give a high quality of personal service and aims its marketing at only the 'self-esteem' section of human need – but units of this type will become more and more expensive to operate and therefore room rates will continue to escalate. The multi-purpose unit may, however, represent a better attempt to satisfy the needs of the larger market than the 'chains' are presently doing.

They still must, however, be managed according to the philosophies outlined throughout this book or they will fail. They must have built into them focal points for people to meet or see other people and management and staff must continue to make 'contact'.

This will become more and more difficult as mechanization increases. There are certainly many ways in which the computer can alleviate the shortage of labour in hotels (room service is one which comes to mind) but if this does come to pass then the management priority of human contact will become even more important and meaningful.

18 Changing Direction

What conclusions are we able to draw from all of this? At the beginning of this book I promised to suggest some new directions, some new behaviour that might now appropriately be adopted by the industry. Maybe these new directions are, by now, obvious to the reader of the foregoing – they are certainly straightforward. In the first place they are concerned with how we educate and secondly with how our major hotel corporations expect hotel managers to manage.

It is difficult to determine whether industry has led the educators astray or vice versa. That is to say, has industry demanded a breed of hotel administrators or have the educators merely bred them without regard to the needs of industry? Whichever came first, they are certainly being used. The result, as we have examined earlier, has not been a great success. Standards of hotel service are clearly no higher in so many ways than they were before the massive and universal efforts of today's and yesterday's educators. It is time for educators therefore to recognize the results of their labours. It is time for them to put a stop to the drift away from practical training towards theory and to reintroduce large doses of practical skills training and experience into their programmes.

We have seen that a good leader must be a model to his employees. A good model commands the respect of his 'followers' through being technically competent in the skills required to do the 'follower's' job. The future student cannot command respect when he moves to a supervisory position unless he has had exposure and practice in the basic skills of the business. No hotel management student should be allowed to graduate from a college or university unless he has put in a substantial amount of time learning and practising the basic skills of food and beverage purchasing, production and service. So much of the rest of the industry he has chosen relates to job content; in the case of food and beverage production and service it also relates to *skill*. The time to learn these skills is at the beginning of an hotel career because if they are not learned then, a whole host of status and economic reasons will prevent them ever being learned and the individual manager will be at a disadvantage forever – as will his guests. For this reason the importance of skills training in the colleges and universities should not be played down as being of primary importance. Another advantage of this will be that students will have a real taste of much of what the industry is really all about and the 'men' will soon be sorted from the 'boys'.

The time has also come for hotel educators to consider their *raison d'être* – the hotel guest. The importance of the hotel guest, his requirements and his desires must be re-examined in the syllabi that are taught. Behavioural educators must not only concentrate on man management but must focus, as well, upon 'guest management'. The role of the guest in the industry has been underplayed; it must be re-elevated to the top of the list. The guest, after all, eventually pays the salary of the educator as well as the hotelier. More prominence should be given to the importance and nature of the guest and, at the very least, the word should be reintroduced to the school syllabi.

I cannot help feeling, however, that the major problems lie within the industry itself and within the mould it has itself created. It is corporate requirements that have created the administrative manager and administrative managers have now taken control of corporations and furthered the cause of their own breed. Administrative corporate executives breed administrative corporate executives because they respond to each other's needs.

During recent seminar activity in several countries around the world I carried out an exercise to plot the hours spent in hotels by city hotel managers and the hours spent in city hotels by the guests. The results were fairly similar each time I attempted the exercise and could be dramatically displayed in the following figure.

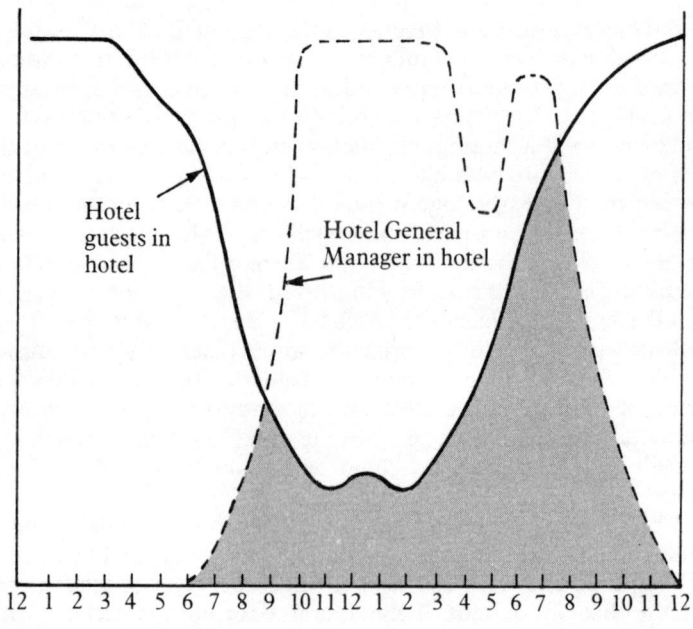

[Figure: Graph showing "Hotel guests in hotel" (solid line, high at midnight, dropping through morning, low during day, rising in evening) versus "Hotel General Manager in hotel" (dashed line, present roughly 7am to 6pm with a dip around 4-5pm), plotted over 24 hours from Midnight to Midnight.]

It is immediately obvious that hotel managers spend the predominant amount of their working time at the hotel when the predominant portion of the clients are elsewhere. I am not suggesting, of course, that hotel managers should only be at the hotel when most of the guests are but I do advocate that hotel companies pay closer attention to the hours that their managers are required to work and to what their managers are doing or are required by the company to be doing during the brief periods when their presence coincides with the presence of their guests.

Clearly the 'crossover' periods are of vital importance. The hotel manager must be disciplined to be in guest contact areas when the guests are actually there. The hotel company must not require the manager to perform administrative functions at the wrong time of day.

Picture the hotel corporation where the central office staff are driving to work, mentally planning their first actions when they arrive in the corporate office. There is an excellent chance that one of them will want to call a hotel unit manager to ask a question or give an instruction. The call will probably be placed between 8 am and 9 am. The hotel manager will have to go to his office (if he is not already in it) to answer the query – just at the time he should be seeing his guests.

A clear understanding of the priorities of the business from the central office through to the supervisors, a common goal, a setting of 'guest contact' disciplines will help to increase customer satisfaction. There is plenty of time for paperwork – but it must be done at the right time. The administrators should not have the upper hand; the guests must!

Surprisingly, technology, for once, is on the side of the guest-oriented hotelier. Until fairly recently the preparation of accounts and budgets was an exceptionally tedious and time-consuming, but very necessary, affair. Now, with the advent of cheaper computers, manual and mental arithmetic can be practically eliminated, leaving far more time for a manager to concentrate on the standards. Administrative corporations must not be allowed to grab this newly-won and valuable time to inject more paper requirements on to the manager. They must use the extra time to the advantage of the guest. Managers must be ejected from the office. The door to the manager's office should be automatically locked (with him *outside*!) during peak periods of guest activity.

If you are just embarking on a career in the hotel industry may I take the liberty of saying that you have chosen well. The hotel industry surely offers one of the most international, interesting, and rewarding careers for which an individual can ask. The real reward, however, comes from a pride in the standards you are able to achieve and the words of thanks and praise that you receive from your clients, even if they 'vote' for you with their feet. The issues raised in the foregoing chapters have all been experienced by the author. They are not meant, nor do they purport to be, a complete dossier on hotel management for there are many, many more aspects to the subject that have not even been touched upon. They are designed, however, to give the reader an overview of many of the behavioural items that have touched me in my particular career. I do hope that the sharing of them will have been of some use to those of you who are working at the moment, or who are about to try.

Bibliography

1 **Berman, Shelley,** *A Hotel is a Place,* (Price, Stern, Sloan, 1972)
2 **Blake, R. R. and Mouton, J. S.,** *The Managerial Grid,* (Gulf, 1964)
3 **Bradford L. P., Gibb, J. R., Benne, K. D.** *'T' Group Theory and Laboratory Methods,* (Wiley, 1966)
4 **Friedland D., Israel R., and Lynch E.,** *People, Productivity in Retailing,* (Lebhar-Friedman Books, 1980)
5 **Goldstein, A. P., and Sorcher, M.,** *Changing Supervisor Behaviour,* (Pergamon Press, 1974)
6 **Likert, Rensis,** *The Human Organisation, (McGraw-Hill, 1967)*
7 **McGregor, Douglas,** *The Human Side of Enterprise,* (McGraw-Hill, 1960)
8 **Nailon, Philip,** *Organisation and Communication,* (University of Surrey, 1968)

Index

Accounting
   timing, 106
   review/analysis, 106
Administration, 30
Administration/mobility scale, 32
Advertising, 117
Appraisals, 113
Asset register, 99
Authoritative management, 54
Automobile industry, 22

Behaviour modelling, 41
'Being there', 31, 32, 33, 64, 86-194
Berman, Shelley, 21, 37
Blake and Mouton, 56
Bradford, Gibb and Benne, 82
Breakfast service, 86
Budgets
   back to zero, 107
   procedures, 107
   capital expenditure, 99

Capital expenditure budger, 99
Carlton Tower Hotel, 80, 83-5
Carlton Hotel, Johannesburg, 118
Cayman Islands, 95
Celebrities, use thereof, 118
Chain hotels, 23
Changing Supervisor Behaviour
   (Goldstein and Sortcher), 42
Chelsea Room, the Carlton Tower, 85
Classroom training, 41
Club Mediterranee, 40, 124
Clothing industry, 22
Colman, John, 22, 125
Communication
   barriers, 39
   developments, 126
   management/staff, 49
   financial information, 51
   styles, 52

Competition, 103
Controller, hotel, 32
Controls, 106
Cosmos, New York, 80
Cultural changes, 30

Departmental barriers, 68
Design, hotels, 23, 122, 123
Detail in modelling, 45
Dissatisfiers, 27
Durban, South Africa, 65
Drucker, Peter, 56

Elangeni Hotel, Durban, 65
Elovic, Albert, 35
Empathy with guests, 105
European hotel schools, 31

Fairfax Hotel, 22
Feedback from guests, 88
Financial goals, 73
First impressions, 103
Focal points in design, 124
Friedland, Israel and Lynch, 48

Georges Cinq Hotel, Paris, 23
Goals and objectives
   balancing, 75
   setting, 74
Goldstein and Sorcher, 42
Grosvenor House Hotel, 108
Guest contact, 35, 36
Guest questionnaires, 105
Guest satisfaction needs, 75

Harris, Kerr, Foster, 76
Hierarchy of needs (Maslow), 18-22, 117
Herzberg, Frederick, 25, 66, 67
Hilton International Hotels, 23
Holiday Inns, 117
Hotel is a Place (a) (Berman), 21

Hotel Corporation of America
  (Sonesta), 81
Housekeeping/reception interfaces, 69
Human Organisation (The) (Likert), 63
Human resource goals, 75
Human Side of Enterprise (The)
  (McGregor), 54
Hyatt Hotels, 22, 23
Hygiene/motivation theory, 25-7
Hynes, James, 80, 83

Industrial Society, The, 84
Ideal hotel manager, 32
Induction, 51
Inn on the Park, 128
Inspection tours, 98,99
Institute for Social Research, 56
Intercontinental Hotels Co., 23
Interfaces between personnel, 68
Interfaces – marketing/operations, 119
Inter-hotel information, 103

Job satisfaction, 66, 67
Job titles, 80
Johari window, 37-9

Kerzner, Sol, 117
Kitchen design, 123
Kitchen/restaurant interfaces, 68

Landdrost Hotel, Johannesburg, 118
Large hotels, 22
Lausanne Hotel School, 44
Laventhol and Horwath, 76
Learning skills, 41
Lighting levels 97
Likert, Rensis, 56-62
Lobby design, 23
Locke, Cartledge and Knerr, 77

McGregor, Douglas, 54
Management by Objectives, 73, 113, 78
Managerial Grid (The) (Blake and
  Mounton, 56
Management systems (Likert),
Market position, 117
Marketing, 74,116
Marketing goals, 74
Maslow, Abraham, 19, 20,21,22,
  25, 117

Mauritius, 47
Milan, Italy, 65, 123
Mobile managers, 108
Model characteristics, 41
Modelling display characteristics, 41
Motivation, 23
Muhammud Ali (boxer), 123
Music levels, 97

Nailon, Philip, 80, 83
Navarro Hotel, 22
New York, 123
Noise levels, 97

Observation skills, 95-9
Observer characteristics, 43
Omni Hotels, 23
Opening hotels, 70, 71
Organization chart, 79
Organisation and Communication
  (Nailon), 84
Origins of hotels, 30
Outside impressions, 102

Par stocks, 107
Paris, 123
Park Lane, London, 80
Parking, importance thereof, 88
Participative management, 54
Penta Hotel, 128
People, Productivity in Retailing
  (Friedland, Israel and Lynch), 48
Peak activity periods, 86
Pele (footballer), 80
Personnel
  administration, 114
  function, 110
  interviewing, 115
  manager, 110
  policing, 113
  recruitment, 115
Physical surveillance, 107
Pilferage, 108
Plaza Hotel New York, 124
Portman, John, 23
Porto Banus, Spain, 35
Post House Hotels, 121
Pre-opening manuals, 70
  planning, 69
  recruitment, 70

Public relations, 74, 119
Pye, Geoff, 80, 83

Reception/housekeeping interfaces, 69
Resort hotels, 93
Restaurants
 ambiance, 97
 interfaces with kitchen, 68
Retailing industry, 48
Rewarding behaviour, 41
Rib Room, The Carlton Tower, 85
Risking communication, 37
Role playing, 41
Room service, 86

Saint Geran Hotel, Mauritius, 47
Saint Louis, 125
Salary increases, 24
Sales force, 119
Santos (footballer), 80
Satisfiers, 27
Self-discipline, 96, 97
Sensitivity training, 81
Sincerity of communication, 97
Social reinforcement, 41
Sonnabend, Roger, 82
Sonesta Hotel, Milan, 65
Span of control, 33
Spinks, Leon (boxer), 122
Staff canteens, 109

Status of trainer, 44
Stranger laboratories, 83
Supportive relationships, 64
Swiss hotels, 31, 32
Switzerland, 31

T Group Theory and laboratory Methods
 (Bradford, Gibb and Benne), 82
'T' groups, 81
Target setting, 75
Team building, 83, 112
Telephone service, 103
Temperature controls, 98
Theory X, 54
Theory Y, 55
Time, managers' use thereof, 86
Training, 113
Training programmes, 114
Travel, a management tool, 104

Uniforms, 98
University of Michigan, 56
University of Surrey, 80

Vier Jarvietzeiten Hotel, Hamburg, 23

Wage administration, 114
Westin Hotels, 23
Women executives, 126

MARKETING HOTELS INTO THE 90s
A systematic approach to increasing sales
Melvyn Greene
Foreword by Sir Maxwell Joseph

'The ultimate in marketing is to establish brand loyalty so that, eventually, not only does the consumer purchase the goods/service once, but continuously' says Melvyn Greene. He goes on to show every hotelier how to improve their business by increasing awareness of consumer demands and by effective marketing. His analysis of social trends and their effects on areas of growth and development is an important feature of the book and will persuade any executive to take a fresh look at his own operation to achieve maximum benefit from new marketing opportunities.

Contents include: main aspects of successfull marketing; planning more than one year ahead; marketing and redefining markets; the eighties and nineties; market segmentation over the next decade; what motivates people to buy; selling — general comments; sales action plans; increasing in-house sales; using names; management information— marketing; improving sales technique; advertising — paid; unpaid advertising — free publicity; sales letters and mailing shots; telephone selling; new forms of selling; face to face selling; conclusion — the threshold barrier.
434 90682 4/360pp/cased

A MANUAL OF STAFF MANAGEMENT IN THE HOTEL AND CATERING INDUSTRY
J. Philip Magurn
Senior Training Adviser, Hotel and Catering Industry Training Board
REVISED REPRINT

The revised reprint of this manual which was designed to provide practical answers to fundamental questions takes into account changes introduced by the Employment Protection (Consolidation) Act, 1978 and also includes a resumé of the Employment Act 1980.

For busy line managers in all sectors of the hotel and catering industry, this book offers a basis for sound staff management practice. Students, following courses leading to:

degrees, diplomas, and professional qualifications in hotel and catering studies

will find it a welcome companion to their textbook reading with its emphasis throughout on practical application and examples.

'A valuable hand refernece for the busy line Catering Manager and exceptionally good value.' *Hospital Caterer.*

1980/222 × 143mm/350pp/434 91198 4

A MANUAL OF HOTEL RECEPTION
J. R. S. Beavis
Professor of Hotel and Catering Management, University of Strathclyde
and S. Medlik
Consultant to the Hotel, Catering and Leisure Industries
Third edition prepared with
R. A. Pullen

The hotel reception office is the main sales outlet of an hotel. It is also a nerve centre of the whole hotel—supplying other departments with information, maintaining liaison with them, and contributing greatly to the overall co-ordination of hotel hospitality. This highly practical manual sets out clearly the principles, methods, systems, and procedures of hotel reception. Its contents have been found applicable to many different types of hotel, from transit to residential, and from city to country and resort hotels.

The third edition has been revised and up-dated to include modern developments, including computer applications to hotel reception and related activities. The text is supported by many new illustrations and an extended series of 20 appendixes. It will be invaluable to students on hotel reception courses and trainees, as well as those on diploma and degree courses in Britain and other countries. It will continue to have a strong appeal for the many thousands of receptionists who have learnt their work 'on the job' and the large body of hotelmen who are always interested in different ideas in hotel reception.

1981/434 91247 6/224pp

THE BUSINESS OF HOTELS
S. Medlik
Consultant to the Hotel,
Catering and Leisure Industries

In this book Professor Medlik, a well known and experienced author, comprehensively examines the hotel as a business providing commercial hospitality. Its focus is on markets, money and people, and the text is illustrated throughout from hotel operations in most parts of the world. Separate chapters are devoted to hotel policies, the main hotel services, organization, staffing and productivity, the small hotel, hotel groups, and international hotel operations.

For the student and teacher of hotel management the whole book and each of its chapters provide an international framework within which the hotel business may be examined at professional, diploma and degree level (for example, in Britain, in HCIMA, HND and degree courses in hotel management).

For the practitioner — the owner, director or manager, the book can help to organize and formalize what he might have already learnt in pracitce and newcomers to hotels and others with a professional interest in understanding them, should find the book a suitable introcuction to their working.

1980/434 91249 2/192pp